Fathers of Conscience

STUDIES IN THE LEGAL HISTORY OF THE SOUTH
Edited by Paul Finkelman, Timothy S. Huebner, and Kermit L. Hall

This series explores the ways in which law has affected the development of the southern United States and in turn the ways the history of the South has affected the development of American law. Volumes in the series focus on a specific aspect of the law, such as slave law or civil rights legislation, or on a broader topic of historical significance to the development of the legal system in the region, such as issues of constitutional history and of law and society, comparative analyses with other legal systems, and biographical studies of influential southern jurists and lawyers.

BERNIE D. JONES

Fathers of

Mixed-Race Inheritance in the Antebellum South

Conscience

The University of Georgia Press *Athens & London*

Acknowledgments for previously published materials appear on
page xiii, which constitutes an extension of the copyright page.

© 2009 by the University of Georgia Press
Athens, Georgia 30602
www.ugapress.org
All rights reserved
Designed by Walton Harris
Set in 10.5/14 New Baskerville
Printed and bound by Thomson-Shore

The paper in this book meets the guidelines for permanence
and durability of the Committee on Production Guidelines
for Book Longevity of the Council on Library Resources.

Printed in the United States of America

13   12   11   10   09   C   5   4   3   2   1
13   12   11   10   09   P   5   4   3   2   1

Library of Congress Cataloging-in-Publication Data

Jones, Bernie D.
Fathers of conscience : mixed-race inheritance in the
antebellum South / Bernie D. Jones.
       p.   cm.
Includes bibliographical references and index.
ISBN-13: 978-0-8203-2980-2 (hardcover : alk. paper)
ISBN-10: 0-8203-2980-0 (hardcover : alk. paper)
ISBN-13: 978-0-8203-3251-2 (pbk. : alk. paper)
ISBN-10: 0-8203-3251-8 (pbk. : alk. paper)
1. Racially mixed people—Legal status, laws, etc.—Southern
States—History—19th century. 2. Illegitimate children—Legal
status, laws, etc.—Southern States—History—19th
century. 3. Women slaves—Legal status, laws, etc.—Southern
States—History—19th century. 4. Wills—Southern
States—Cases. 5. Inheritance and succession—Social
aspects—Southern States—History—19th century. 6. Men,
White—Family relationships—Southern States—History—19th
century. 7. Slaveholders—Family relationships—Southern
States—History—19th century. 8. Slaves—Family
relationships—Southern States—History—19th century.
9. Social classes—Southern States—History—19th century.
10. Southern States—Race relations—History—19th century.
KF4755 .J66 2009
342.7508'7—dc22   2008043133

British Library Cataloging-in-Publication Data available

For the Women

CONTENTS

I FIRST BECAME INTERESTED in this topic of miscegenation and antebellum will contests when I was a doctoral candidate at the University of Virginia. I had passed my comprehensive exams and was getting ready to teach my first classes. Searching for a topic, I researched as much as I could on African Americans and the law in the hope of offering such a class to students at the Carter G. Woodson Institute at the university.

Paul Finkelman's book *An Imperfect Union: Slavery, Federalism and Comity* introduced me to a story that fascinated me, the case of *Mitchell v. Wells*. An enslaved woman named Nancy Wells had been freed by her owner, who was also her father. Sending her to Ohio from Mississippi, she lived there before he died. In his will he left her various items—a bed, a watch, and three thousand dollars. When she claimed her bequest, other beneficiaries, including the executor, who was also her cousin, said she should not inherit because she was a slave. In an 1859 opinion, the Mississippi High Court of Errors and Appeals agreed with her opponents. Under Mississippi law she was a slave with no rights to inherit, even though she was an Ohio resident and a free woman of color. Not understanding the full context of the law of slavery, I wondered whether she had been legally reenslaved. I decided I would eventually research her case further and then write about it.

But I had a dissertation to write, so Nancy Wells's story landed on a back burner for a handful of years, until I was finishing a postdoctoral fellowship and about to take a faculty position at the University of Massachusetts–Amherst. Reading materials on the case, I struggled to think about what I could say about the case that had not been said already. Thanks to Professor Finkelman's guidance, I found a far broader, interesting and viable approach. He suggested I think about how judges who heard cases such as *Mitchell v. Wells* responded to the evidence of miscegenation indicated by the wills, the challenges that followed, and the testimony presented by witnesses. How were the men seen at the time?

Reading appellate decisions reported from throughout the South in which testators' last wills were challenged, I aimed to discover whether there were patterns indicated in the judicial and community responses to cases in which miscegenation had been alleged. I found that the testators tended to be single or widowed men who left significant bequests to enslaved women and their children. In these cases there was no white wife or legitimate white child to take the inheritance. As a result, white relatives asserted the wills were invalid, hoping to deny the women and children their inheritance. The cases discussed here indicate, then, the extent to which various southern states developed a jurisprudence of inheritance rights across the color line.

Thus began what has been an engrossing project. I soon realized, however, just why this project was important. Essie Mae Washington came forward in December 2003, claiming to be the daughter of the late Senator Strom Thurmond, one-time ardent segregationist and opponent of African American civil rights. The public responded with shock, and in some instances, with disbelief. How could he have fathered a child by a family maid while a young man, supported her financially, yet never acknowledged her officially? How was he able to keep it secret?

What many might not have realized is that secrecy was at the heart of cases such as the Williams-Thurmond case and is part of an aspect of southern culture going back to the antebellum period and slavery. White men who had children by enslaved women and free women of color were not legally obligated to care for such children. Enslaved women were not allowed to marry, and their out-of-wedlock children were deemed to be their mothers' children, not their fathers'. Their parents' relations, consensual or not, were secrets not openly acknowledged by society, except behind the veils of gossip.

But the men at the heart of the cases of contested wills did not keep secrets. They left behind last wills and testaments that became part of the public record. These indicated they had children by enslaved women; they hoped to recognize them all by liberating the mothers, their children, and finally, giving them property. The appellate decisions generated by their cases comprise a treasure trove of material for the historian interested in property law, the law of slavery, trusts and estates law, and the legal culture of the antebellum South. This book explores different legal cultures of slavery through a focus on the cases as presented and argued by the parties to the actions, and the judicial opinions influenced by the state legislative and constitutional cultures that shaped them, combined with the judges' individual perceptions of slavery and manumission.

In undertaking this project I was fortunate to receive generous encouragement and support. I would first like to thank my colleagues at the University of Massachusetts–Amherst. In the Department of Legal Studies: Steve Arons, Eve Darian-Smith, Alan Gaitenby, Tom Hilbink, Judith Holmes, Ethan Katsh, Amity Lee-Bradley, Tami Paluca, Ron Pipkin, Leah Wing, and Diana Yoon; Dean Janet Rifkin and Provost Charlena Seymour; the members of the Law and Society Initiative; the participants in the Interdisciplinary Seminar in Humanities and the Fine Arts, "Marriage and its Alternatives," particularly Susan Shapiro. Special thanks also to Barbara Morgan, reference librarian; Arlene Avakian in Women's Studies; Nilanjana Dasgupta in psychology; Laura Lovett, history; and Francoise Hamlin, formerly in the History Department, but now at Brown University; and Mary McClintock. Colleagues from outside the university include Al Brophy, Laura Edwards, Tanya K. Hernandez, L. Brown Kennedy, Charles W. McCurdy (my former advisor), Lucy Salyer, and the faculty at Suffolk University School of Law. Thanks also to those at the University of Georgia Press, especially Nancy Grayson, the anonymous reader, the editorial board, and Deborah Oliver, editor.

I presented earlier versions of the manuscript at various venues, and parts of it were previously published in "Righteous Fathers, Vulnerable Old Men and Degraded Creatures: Southern Justices on Miscegenation in the Antebellum Will Contest," 40 *Tulsa Law Review* 699–750 (summer 2005). Thanks to the participants in the fall 2004 Legal History Symposium at the University of Tulsa School of Law; the fall 2004 Baylor Institute for Faith and Learning conference, Slavery and Oppression; the Elizabeth Battelle Clark Legal History Series, Boston University School of Law, spring 2005; the J. Willard Hurst Legal History Summer Institute in the summer of 2005; and the Southern Association for Women Historians in the summer of 2006.

I was grateful for the financial support of the Institute for Southern Studies at the University of South Carolina to do research at the university library and at the South Carolina Department of Archives and History. Steve Tuttle at the archives was particularly helpful.

Receiving the William Nelson Foundation fellowship in Legal History was an honor that provided research support for traveling to archives. I received able help from the staff at the New England Historic Genealogical Society; the Mississippi Department of Archives and History; Trinity College library, Hartford, Connecticut; Yale Sterling Memorial Library and the Kentucky Department of Library and Archives, especially Lisa Thompson. Thanks also to those at the Kentucky Historical Society, the University of Kentucky Special Collections, Transylvania University, and Dolores Salsman in the Nelson County Clerk's Office, Kentucky. Receiving an American Association of University Women Short-term Research Publication Grant was helpful in preparing the manuscript for publication.

As I was finishing the manuscript I looked for an image that would encapsulate the theme of this study—mixed-race slaves, miscegenation, parenthood, and family—and what came to mind was a painting I'd seen years ago in a New York City museum exhibit. Colleagues on one of the H-net Listservs helped me identify Thomas Satterwhite Noble's *The Price of Blood*, which appears on the cover of the paperback and in the introduction. Thanks to the Morris Museum of Art, Augusta, Georgia, for permission to use the image, for this study is truly about the price of blood: just what was it worth to emancipate or oppose the liberation of blood relatives?

Important throughout everything have been friends and family, the people who asked how things were going, who were curious about what I was working on, and who wished me well: my parents, Michael and Eliza Jones, Francis and Kelli Phillip, Karen Francis, Evelyn Hercules, Magnola Purcell-Hunt, Louisa and Delbert Bauldock, Elizabeth Noel and family, Rose McMahan, Erin Berard, Pat Boyd, Cherie Lewis, Nicole Hudgins, Joy Asekun, Colette Dabney, and those at Grace Episcopal Church–Amherst. Finally, special thanks are due my husband, Daniel A. Perrault, for all his support.

Fathers of Conscience

When a white man freed an enslaved woman and her children in his
will, for example, did that mean he found her lifelong service worth
the reward of emancipation, or did the manumission conceal a more
intimate relationship?

—JOSHUA D. ROTHMAN, *Notorious in the Neighborhood*

Inheritance Rights in the Antebellum South

THIS BOOK CONSIDERS HOW WHITES of the antebellum South
negotiated inheritance rights when slave beneficiaries were related
by blood to their late owners. Were slave owners who partnered
with enslaved black women and who fathered mixed-race children
able to manumit in their wills and grant property to the women and
children? How did the men's white relatives react to such bequests?
When judges hearing cases of contested wills responded in the appellate courts, what type of language did they use in describing the
men? How did that use of language determine whether the wills
would stand? What was the influence of changing manumission requirements over time on judicial decision making?

The answers to all these questions lay in how state court judges of the antebellum South resolved competing demands: an owner's right to relinquish property balanced against the community's interest in the enslavement and subordination of blacks. The strategies the men pursued—manumission during life or upon death—were ultimately influenced, then, by more than the law of slavery as found in state constitutional provisions and legislative enactments. The men gambled on whether trial court judges, juries, and appellate courts would uphold their attempts to use trusts and estates law. The fates of women and children were at stake. Would they be able to obtain freedom and property through their ties of privilege and access to whiteness? Individual judges on the state high courts based their decisions on their own perceptions of white southern manhood, fatherhood, property rights, and the social good of the white community.

Slave owners in the antebellum South who sought to liberate and alienate property to enslaved women and the children the women bore acted as both insiders and outsiders when they used the law. These slaveholders were the ultimate insiders, white men empowered by the law to be owners of slaves and of land. But their alliances made them into outsiders by forcing them to use trusts and estates law in unique ways as legislatures modified the law of slavery during the course of the antebellum period, changing constitutional provisions and passing legislation that made manumission more difficult. They became outsiders because they affirmed allegiances to blacks in rejection of white interests to retain property within the white community and to deny blacks their freedom.

State court judges who heard cases of contested wills involving bequests to the putative enslaved partners and children of slaveholding white men exercised their power to decide when social boundaries had been breached. As we shall see, in the view of the greater society miscegenation between white men and enslaved women or free women of color was not a problem. Instead, the color line was breached when white men recognized and accorded enslaved women and their mixed-race children status in white society by bequeathing them property and manumitting them. Official recognition by white relatives meant access to whiteness; black personal freedom, combined with access to money and land, was a threat to the social order

Thomas Satterwhite Noble, *The Price of Blood*. 1868, oil on canvas, 39¼ × 49½ inches. Morris Museum of Art, Augusta, Georgia

of slavery and white supremacy. Free blacks, particularly when they had money, were deemed uncontrollable, arrogant, and a bad influence on the bonded. In the eyes of jurists who ascribed to this view, wealthy free black status was to be denied at all costs, for the benefit of the white social order and the white relatives or creditors seeking to establish their claims to the decedent's estate.

Contrary to this view of the law of slavery consistently being used to reinforce the demands of the slave order, other jurists supported the efforts of slave owners to atone for their transgressions; the men were fulfilling a moral obligation to the women and children.[1] Perhaps as Thomas Morris has noted, the "analytic model" proposed by Mark Tushnet does not consider "the messy and often complex attempts of Southern judges to deal with the problems created by 'thinking property.'"[2] The needs and demands of the greater social order were not as important in the view of some judges, compared to the prerogatives of the individual owner to relinquish his slave property and divide his estate as he wished. It is important to note, though, that notwithstanding an interest among these judges to uphold the rights of individual white men and their black families, these judges who supported manumission and the granting of bequests should not be seen as abolitionists. They were men of their time and place who believed in the social order of slavery, and they might have been slave owners themselves.

It is important to note that all of the judges hearing such cases were faced with a paradox stemming from competing moral perspectives of owner–slave relations. Slavery, as a cultural and social institution, was reinforced by religion and the secular law. Although the judges did not cite scriptural verses, they used biblical language to justify their decisions. According to these southern Protestants, the Bible recognized slavery as a practice, providing justification for pro-slavery judges to promote its existence. Moreover, the Bible could be used to rationalize the separation of the races and the subordination of the African. Yet the Bible could also be used to justify improving the condition of slaves or even to condemn slavery, as the northern Protestant abolitionists did. Thus in the eyes of judges who upheld the rights of enslaved women and their children, slavery was an unfortunate aspect of southern society. It was a distasteful but necessary practice, instrumental for white wealth and the proper ordering of the society their ancestors had developed since the colonial period. But slavery also called upon these judges to exercise their greatest humanity, insofar as their treatment of enslaved women and mixed-race enslaved children indicated benevolence.

These two impulses came into conflict in the will contest. On the one hand, moralism—one's sense of proper moral behavior—could tend toward righteous indignation: criticism of testators for sinning, committing adultery and crossing color lines. On the other hand, moralism could view care for former enslaved partners and children as an example of pious atonement for sin and as fathers' fulfillment of obligations to mothers and children. Whether an individual judge was willing to let a testator do as he wished thus depended not only on the law of slavery but on the judge's position on personal and social responsibility. Were owners who had sex with their slaves sinful?

If their behavior was sinful, should a slave owner be able to provide for "the fruit of his sin," his enslaved child? What obligations did a judge have to the legal and social orders of a slave society? Should a judge use the law of wills to punish a testator's moral failures, his fornication with slaves, or was punishment solely a matter to be addressed by religious institutions? What responsibilities did slaveholders have to themselves, their slaves, and the white community?

Yet the morality question need not always be a driving factor, nor need opinions on slavery's role in society be a motivation. In the view of some judges on the appellate courts, those political questions did not always matter. Instead, the plain "black letter" law could have determined whether a will would stand. The precedents just might have favored the decedent, and the judges felt obligated to follow stare decisis. They were obligated to decide in light of the common law until the legislature passed a statute or a constitutional amendment that said otherwise. When all these were favorable and led to upholding the wills, the end result then was a decision favorable to the inheritance interests of the women and children.

The judicial power to determine the validity of wills was not to be taken lightly. As arbiters of the law, men of business and property would have looked to them for guidance on whether and how to manumit by will. This applied to both the large-plantation owner and the small farmer, the latter made elite by nature of his slave ownership, for men of both groups left wills that were contested. But, most significantly, the judges set forth the community standards, insofar as they established the parameters of behavior, what white men could do in their personal lives, setting forth which sanctions might or might not follow if social mores were transgressed. Manumission laws passed by legislators determined whether a white man could provide for enslaved women and their children during his lifetime, but judges hearing will contests decided whether he could provide for them upon his death.

State court judges heard appeals from local trial courts and set the standard lower court judges and lawyers would follow in making arguments and determinations. They guided jurors in explaining how they should view constructions of fact in light of the law. In the case of slave owners seeking to use the law of wills in providing for partners and enslaved children when the law of slavery barred legal remedies or made them difficult to pursue, the high-court judges were called upon to arbitrate various interests: the testator's desire to do what he thought was proper versus the community's interest in upholding slavery and retaining white wealth, under the guise of punishing immoral behavior. Of significance was whether a judge was willing to respect testators' property rights.

Deciding to uphold a will and manumit was not merely about the legal issues limited to the case at hand. Each case presented the judge with political implications and tensions to be resolved. As slavery died and abolitionist fervor increased in the North, southerners felt forced to defend their institution of slavery, and will contests point to how the judges responded to one aspect of the growing debate. Perhaps societal respect for the paternalism of individual testators should be encouraged, providing an example to abolitionists that slavery was not so terrible because slave owners were benevolent patriarchs. Or, perhaps the judges should deny manumissions altogether, as a forceful response to the growing abolition movement. It could also be that the judges themselves were facing a conflict over their own role: how would they be seen in the eyes of others as they tried to negotiate competing demands? Were they willing to protect these fathers, the enslaved women and their children, or were they overturning the religiously ordained system of slavery by rewarding fornication across color lines? Were the persons named in the cases before them victims worthy of protection under the law?

The matter of sexual relations between slave owners and enslaved women had long been a controversial one. Statutory law did not make white men liable to prosecution for sexual contact with female slaves, and under the law, the children of enslaved women were slaves from birth, regardless of the fathers' status; the fathers were not bound by law to support such children. The women in question were not white women who had greater rights under the social and legal orders. A white woman could claim rape or ravishment. Community pressure could be brought upon a white man to marry the white woman he was alleged to have seduced. If a white married man died intestate, his white widow was automatically entitled under common law to dower, a third of her husband's estate. Enslaved women had no such entitlements. When slave owners recognized in their wills enslaved women and their mixed-race children, intending that they become free, state law could force them to remain in bondage. They could be denied the property they were meant to have for their upkeep and support, something that would have never been done to married white mothers and legitimate white children.

Without the law to force their obligations to the enslaved women who bore them children, only the men's consciences and fear of public scorn held sway over the men's behavior. But even if their activities were known, public scorn might not even follow, in that they were not answerable to anyone, because the men were unmarried or widowed. But the community was in an uproar once the men died and their last wills were read. Granted bequests of freedom and property by their owners, the enslaved women and their mixed-race enslaved children then became caught up in the machinations of white creditors and relatives who were seeking to deny their access to property, in a society in which access to property and owning it was a hallmark of whiteness.

The claimants' greed was fueled by racism, as was their use of the language of morality, which had great social currency and which resonated among judges on the bench. The language of shame could frame the judicial response in the ways challengers might have hoped, but this was not always successful. The language thus indicated a dualism in the sense that atonement for sin could be found through a will and justified in decisions granting bequests of freedom and property, alongside the language of shame used as a postmortem punishment for transgressions and denial of a testator's will. Those judges who sought a "humane" slavery were likely to view providing for enslaved children as atonement for sin and shame. I use the term "humane" here to describe the rationale given by various judges for explaining why the testators' wishes should be fulfilled: recognition of slaves' humanity might deflect criticism that slavery was inhumane. As William E. Wiethoff explains, a "humane" slavery represented a balance: "Addresses to humanity and interest—the moral imperative to treat slaves humanely and the South's interest in maintaining slavery."[3]

Those who were far more interested in punishing dead testators and denying rewards to slave beneficiaries focused more on defining testators who crossed the color line as immoral. Not only were these testators reprehensible for having engaged in extramarital sexual relations, but they were immoral for having contributed to social upheaval. Ultimately, the tensions among the judges lay in conflicts over how they saw their duty to decide upon cases where moral, but not legal, transgressions were at stake: out-of-wedlock sex with enslaved women combined with the granting of bequests of freedom and property to them and the children born of their unions. At issue was whether white heirs should inherit estates, notwithstanding testators' desire to provide for enslaved partners and children. Law and public policy could thus cut two ways: protect the rights of all testators not to have their wishes ignored, or support slavery first and foremost.

My purpose is not to romanticize by arguing that these relations were consensual and affectionate, or to romanticize the women's and children's struggles to gain inheritances. It is unclear how much power enslaved women had in their relationships to negotiate for freedom and property for themselves and their children. These were women living under conditions of extreme domination based on their race and gender. If they did not submit to their owners, their lives or the lives of others could be threatened. Moreover, the notion of autonomy is undercut by their lack of legal standing in the lawsuits. In many instances the enslaved women were minor actors, mere property, pawns in a power play among whites over the terms of a will, because the women had no inheritance rights. The enslaved women at the heart of these actions were not parties to the action although they might have been named in the will, they had no legal capacity, and therefore could not testify in their own defense: their fates would be decided by whites. When not maligning them as controlling jezebels, drunkards, and prostitutes, white witnesses testified to the existence of partnerships: enslaved women managing households who seemed to live on some level of social equality with their white male owners.

Even when the testators explained in their wills that their relationships were consensual, without knowing the day-to-day relations and perspectives of all participants, it is impossible to verify such arguments. The men's relations with the women were tainted by slavery: his empowerment compared to her disempowerment. Could a woman under those circumstances ever have the right to say no? The men had the power to coerce, and as Adrienne Davis noted in her study of slavery and sexual harassment law, enslaved women's work spaces and home spaces were intertwined: sexual labor and sexual abuse could be part of each.[4] It is impossible today to divine the nature of the enslaved women's relationships with the powerful white men who controlled their lives and to know whether, in a system in which marriage between the races was illegal, the women were rape victims or life partners.

It also remains beyond our knowledge whether the women gained power through their sexual contacts with the men. In testimony in which the enslaved women beneficiaries were seen as powerful jezebels, whites presumed that the women had a certain level of agency to coerce the men without them having to acknowledge that sexual access was no guarantee of power. Instead of manipulating their owners, their owners could have manipulated them. Blandishments could be ignored and promises forgotten in the face of relationships grounded in dominance and hierarchy. So even if an enslaved woman hoped to benefit from a sexual relationship with her owner, without moral authority, social practice, or the law binding the men to any obligation to the women, there would have been no guarantee that she would get what she wanted. Thus what ultimately mattered most is what the law set forth: enslaved black women were personal property capable of being used and moved from one location to the next. Excluded from the presumption of chastity and due no protection of their sexuality because of their race, they were vulnerable to sexual abuse and exploitation.

Even though the women in the cases I examine were mothers, they might have been invisible parties to the action, present only through the fruit of their sexual activity. Their children were suing for their right to become free people of color, but it was as though their mothers did not exist. This happened because the legal system forced the enslaved women's children to minimize or deny their black mothers, for to claim rights through their fathers' wills they had to present themselves as though they had no other parent. Their fathers' behavior might have even modeled that fiction. The men were their owners with sole control over their lives and the lives of their mothers. The women's status as property under the law enabled this, thus the women were known by a first name only, or were altogether nameless and faceless. The men decided who they wanted to favor, and this created tensions not only within their white families of origin but among their slaves. When property rights to land and cash were at stake, both the women and children were fighting in turn for the rights to claim wealth built by the community of slaves, thereby contributing to even more stratification even as they claimed kinship with their owners.

How then was evidence of miscegenation found? The parties presented the facts at trial or through the statements of witnesses who knew the testator. Slave owners could end the secrecy by speaking through their wills, perhaps circumventing informal rules of denial: acknowledgment of their unions and offspring. But in cases in which the court opinions do not explain the circumstances of a testator's benevolence, one can infer there was more at stake than simple kindness, the goodwill of a patriarch toward his slave "children," slaves deemed childlike yet loyal and obedient, thus earning his munificence.

Particularly noteworthy are cases such as those presented here, where a widowed or single white man made unusual bequests to an enslaved or free woman of color and her children, with no white wife or legitimate white child to take the inheritance. Although he could have manumitted during life and given them property to enjoy as people of color living in free states, he did not pursue that option. Instead, he aimed to have it done by others upon his death. He might have singled out one slave child, described as the child of one of his female slaves, making it clear that the child was not to be considered part of his estate. Instead, the child was to be given special treatment: freedom, education, and money. In jurisdictions in which statutes and case law constrained their ability to manumit, testators sought other means: asking the executors to take the woman and her children to northern states where they might live freely, and setting up trust funds for their support. Another option could include willing them to the American Colonization Society, in order that they might be taken to Africa and become free blacks. The men crafted wills that they hoped would stand. But doing so had its risks. Even when their relationships were well known during their lifetimes, their relatives and the white community did not necessarily accept such relationships. Living with enslaved black women on levels of equality defined them as transgressors of the social order who betrayed their race and class.

Perhaps criticism and ostracism were the only means of exerting social control upon men whose class and race privileges freed them to live their lives as they chose and gave them the ability to use the law at their deaths for distributing their property how they wanted. They had no white wives and children to whom they had legal obligations. In death they were beyond the law's reach for prosecution for miscegenation. But the will contest might have been the means by which their relatives retaliated against these men who had been wayward and disrespectful of white conventions: they insisted on making enslaved women and children the beneficiaries of their bounty. Sex with an enslaved woman was one thing, but giving her property that whites had a legal right to inherit was quite another. The enslaved women relied nonetheless on community members—white men who served on juries, trial court and appellate judges—to uphold the late owners' wills when collateral heirs—parents, siblings, aunts, uncles, nieces, nephews, and cousins—challenged the will.

More often than not, undue influence or incapacity formed the basis of the heirs' claim. In trusts and estates practice the testator sets forth the disposition of the property owned at the time of death. He names an executor he trusts to be able to carry out his wishes. Under normal circumstances the executor presents the will to the probate court and it is accepted. The executor then finds the assets, pays the estate's debts, and sees that the bequests are made as the testator wanted. But when a will is challenged, that process is suspended while a will contest ensues. The challengers to the will could be people named in the will who are challenging particular bequests, or collateral heirs challenging the entire will as void. These collateral heirs are relatives who would inherit under the state's probate law if the will were declared invalid. In the cases discussed in this book, they might have claimed the testators suffered an incapacity that rendered them legally incapable of making a reasonable disposition of the property. In the undue influence cases, claimants argued that testators were in a vulnerable position, reliant upon trusted associates who then induced them to act contrary to their best interests and those of their legitimate white relatives.

But in all the contested-will cases discussed here, appellate judges, not juries, were the arbiters. The attitudes and rulings of these elite jurists of the antebellum South ranged from tolerance of the liaisons their slaveholding brethren had with enslaved black women, to sympathy with these sorrowful sinners trying to do right by their enslaved children, to despising the degraded creatures who succumbed to illicit sex and undermined the whole social order of slavery. Some judges postulated that the testators were insane or arrogant to have denied the interests of their white relatives in order to elevate a slave with freedom and bequests of property. As benighted fools or helpless old men they were the pawns of overly powerful black jezebels who controlled them and their households.

In her book, legal historian Ariela Gross discusses deficient mastery in the context of owners' inadequate management.[5] Owners didn't understand slaves' personalities, couldn't control them, and didn't know how to get them to work effectively. Mastery was also significant in the cases discussed here, though in a different way. In the patriarchal society of the day, these masters were deemed deficient because they did not assert and maintain appropriate boundaries with their female slaves. Other masters had sexual contact with their female slaves but did not become attached or sentimental, and they did not forget their obligations to race and class.

It is significant that many of these cases of contested wills had been decided in the chancery courts at the trial level. The chancellors heard not only cases involving trusts and estates law but cases in equity, when the law courts offered no recourse, and justice was at stake. As a result, when the judges heard appeals from the chancery courts they were called upon to consider what their roles were. The consequences of their decisions fell upon the social and legal orders: tensions within the slave order, empowerment of free blacks, and encouragement of white men to use trusts and estates law in ways the law of slavery never intended. The judges were considering more than the matters of the litigation at hand—long-term policy mattered, too.

In the view of some judges the formal law of slavery, as legislated by the slave codes and developed through case law dating back to the colonial period, was built upon notions of natural law that defined blacks as inferior and not to be elevated to equality with whites; their enslavement fit into the proper ordering of U.S. society. All blacks were to be slaves for life, under the absolute control of an owner, with no right to freedom and no right to own property. As Tushnet described it, when testators violated those natural laws by seeking to manumit through their wills, appellate judges could overturn on policy grounds practices they deemed dangerous to the well-being of society, namely, slaves given freedom and economic equality with whites. Preservation of racial stratification was paramount.[6] Judges who held this view exercised their authority, acting as bulwarks against black upward mobility by denying manumission and the transfer of property from white to black. They established the legal framework within which testators operated. By ruling against testators who left bequests of freedom and property to enslaved women and children, they guided the white community on proper mores: no elevation of blacks to economic equality with whites.

Such judges constrained themselves to narrow, formulaic interpretations of the law of slavery and inheritance rights that demanded denial of black rights as a matter of law and social policy.[7] But judges who aimed to protect testators' prerogatives also had natural law on their side. The right to hold property included the right to relinquish, and as a matter of private law, one could do what one wished with one's property, particularly if there were significant moral obligations at stake, obligations that were also important as a matter of natural law. Patriarchs in a slave regime were called upon to exercise benevolence toward their dependents, their wives, children, and the slaves they owned. If they were unmarried but owned enslaved women who bore their children, masters exercising their moral obligations to care for them should also be able to, because natural law demanded it.

Whether a judge was tolerant or intolerant of owners' prerogatives to provide for the women and children, state slavery laws gave room to deny emancipation and the transfer of property, for the benefit of creditors and white heirs, notwithstanding the intent of the testators and any rights they might have had to resolve their estate as they pleased. In those instances, the social order of slavery was more important. Other judges could also use the formal law of slavery for their own ends, using their discretion and deciding in ways such that fulfilled the testators' intent, notwithstanding the jurisdiction's preference for bondage over freedom. In some instances, those judges had acted as advisors and executors in fulfilling the wishes of their testator clients.

The men had options as a result: access to learned and competent lawyers who were willing to help them write a will that enabled them to fulfill their wishes. Moreover, there were judges on the appellate courts who supported slavery and were just as dedicated to upholding it in all forms, but who were willing to respect the testators' wishes in cases of contested wills where miscegenation had been alleged. Thus one can explain some of the contradictions found in judicial advocates of slavery who nonetheless upheld the rights of enslaved women and children to become free. As elite white men they could not quarrel with other white men's rights to live as they pleased and dispose of their own property as they wished at their death. Judges could vote against their slavery bias and respect the wishes of testators who took their fatherly duties seriously. Those judges freed slaves and gave them the bequests their fathers left them, notwithstanding their disgust at racial mixing and their dislike of an increasing free black population.

An owner could manumit by taking the women and children to a northern state, including those of the old Northwest Ordinance, such as Ohio, then return and draft a will in his home state. This strategy of physically removing them ensured that as free people of color they would be able to sue to protect their rights. These were the strongest legal cases, most likely to result in victory. Through the combination of geographic mobility and the stroke of a pen, the previously bonded could become free, in a paradox of property and power. One moment they were slaves living in the South; the next they were free black northerners with a greater legal potential to inherit.[8]

Not only were the men iconoclasts in refusing to follow the social rules that would deny recognition of enslaved partners and biological children, but when legislatures tightened manumission policies, they employed legal strategies that referred to the private law of wills: trusts and estates law. The judges, in responding to this instrumentalism, were then caught in a bind: should they use their own instrumentalism in support of inheritance law, though doing so would subvert the social order essential to white southerners' existence? Should they deny the men's ingenuity and thus provide precedent to subvert everyone's property rights? For if a white man's rights to property could be subverted based upon subjective evidence, was anyone's property rights safe? Couldn't other white men be labeled and criticized unjustly and their wills challenged, just because their relatives were displeased at the way they devolved their estates?

One might argue that the sale of slaves upon the dissolution of estates or the denial of slaves to own property was not unusual for its time, for under trusts and estates law all debts incurred by decedents must be paid before anyone can inherit, and slaves were personal property to be bought and sold. This was complicated, however, by race and sex: that enslaved black women were rendered powerless by the caste system of slavery. If an enslaved woman and children were both relatives of a testator and property he owned, what happened when they were freed by a will but the estate did not have enough money to pay the debts? The law did not accord them the rights of legitimate white family members—the wives and children who easily inherited money, status, and security from their husbands and fathers. Because they were "illegitimate," they became subjects at the center of will contests in which disgruntled heirs accused them of engaging in the nefarious: forcing white men to give them property to the detriment of legitimate family members.

This book is organized into five chapters that develop the themes of race, gender, and inheritance rights as they affected enslaved women and their children as "illegitimate" heirs. Chapter 1 comprises a study of appellate decisions reported from various state supreme courts, where judges heard cases from the lower courts over questions of law. Such opinions are valuable insofar as they include the factual matters at the heart of the dispute. But most important, they set forth the highest state court authority on interracial matters and demonstrate the interplay between the local trial courts and the high courts in establishing social norms and interpreting legislation. Although most of the decisions involved cases of contested wills, some grew out of commercial lawsuits where the status of free persons of color came into question: were they eligible to conduct business transactions? The questions then turned on how they had become free people of color who owned property. There had been some act of manumission combined with a bequest of property from a will. Insofar as the opinions include testimony from the trial courts, they are a rich source of material on attitudes toward interracial sex and family relationships. Will contests often generate their own drama, and those of the antebellum South were no exception, as judges heard cases that exposed family secrets, rivalries among members, and greed.

White family members fought for all they could get, for the law of slavery tended to support their interests in property, and huge sums of money—real property, cash, securities, and personal property, including the slaves at the heart of the litigation—could be at stake. Moreover, the culture encouraged them to criticize their male relatives who had had sexual relationships with enslaved women that led to grants of freedom and property for the women and their children, because the law did not obligate them to recognize familial ties to the blacks in their midst. The creditors sought to have their debts paid out of the estate, and were quite willing to use the enslaved women and their children to pay, even if the testator's intent was that they not be considered part of the estate.

The executors looked to their responsibilities to fulfill the testators' wishes and protect the women and children, but not always. They sometimes tried to take the proceeds for themselves. The black claimants, when they were parties to the lawsuits, asserted their status as relatives, struggling for what they thought was legitimately theirs: the bequests left to them by the men. And when their white relatives denied their right to freedom, they were fighting for their very lives. In some cases the white family members won, and in others the black relatives did. The judges who disinherited in essence championed slavery and white supremacy, particularly as northern antislavery sentiment increased in the 1830s to 1850s, and as southern legislatures, frightened of an increasing free black population, tightened their manumission laws. Tighter manumission laws meant that judges could defer to the legislature and ignore any sentiments in favor of testators' rights.

In addressing how the judges saw the testators, I examine individual cases and focus on categories of responses, discovering the nuances of judicial behavior, instead of making broad generalizations within and across jurisdictions. A testator could have been described as a virtuous father, a victim, a degenerate, or all at the same time. But most noteworthy was that a judge's interpretation could be different from those of the challengers to the will, which demonstrates the tensions within the slaveholding elite as they grappled with interracial sex and the transfer of property. Where challengers saw vulnerability, a judge might have seen a lucid and rational man of business sure of how he wanted to dispose of his property.

Narrative as found in these cases of contested wills thus drove much of the judicial inquiry because the behavior and actions of the testator prior to his death were under scrutiny. This narrative encompassed not only interpretations of the men as legal actors, but stories about the women and children as developed by the litigants. The men's lifestyles were being called into question. Had they been the victims of overreaching slaves? Did they suffer some from mental incapacity? Could their unorthodox wills have been explained by their blatant transgression of social mores? Were they just fathers trying to take care of their children and former partners? How might the slave order be affected if the will were to stand? All these questions had to be answered, as the judges were negotiating the rights of white men as the partners of enslaved women and the natural fathers of enslaved children, in opposition to the interests of the slave society. Regardless of the reasons the men did what they did, they used legal strategies that opened the legal consciousness of the women and children named as beneficiaries. The men enabled them to develop their own legal narratives and "engage, avoid, or resist the law and legal meanings" once they could sue as free people of color.[9]

Chapter 2 considers cases in which judges focused solely on the formal law of slavery to deny manumission as a matter of internal policy. Judges in these instances justified their opinions based not only upon constitutions and legislative practices, statutes that limited manumission within the jurisdiction, but were concerned about what slavery meant as an institution: a system of labor that arose within the country for the purpose of increasing white wealth and industry through the use of a perpetual laboring class. It was an ancient system used by Western civilizations throughout history. The statutes and legal opinions that reinforced servitude and subordination were significant for maintaining that system of labor. As such, slave owners seeking to manumit through their wills contravened the needs of the greater community, and for that reason the judges decided against manumission.

At the same time, however, there were judges in similar jurisdictions where constitutions and statutory law demanded subservience and control of slaves, but these were more willing to hold in favor of wills that met the formal requirements of ownership: identification of owners, even though the wills also permitted some modicum of freedom. In those cases, slaves had been the beneficiaries of a trust set up by their former owners. Their new owners were trustees pledged to fulfill the late owner's wishes. Although ownership was arguably a mere formality, the fact that an ownership relationship existed had its own ramifications and limitations upon the slaves' rights. In yet other cases, judges were more willing to recognize the rights of free blacks as not always being perilous to the interests of the local white community. As a result, these were less willing to write in favor of reinforcing slavery and denying freedom as a matter of greater social policy. Instead, they considered issues of justice on a case-by-case basis, in typical common-law fashion.

Chapter 2 also tests the popular perception of Louisiana as a multiracial community where mixed-race free blacks occupied the middle ground between whites and slaves. This view proposes that the French instituted a different system of slavery than existed in its English-speaking neighbors. This system of slavery was apparently fairer, granting greater recognition to free blacks, especially those who were of mixed race. These blacks worked as artisans; they owned farms, plantations, and slaves. But how did Louisiana law address the rights of slaves and free blacks named as beneficiaries in wills? As historian Judith Schafer notes, with respect to manumission and inheritance, Louisiana was not much different from other southern states: limited protection of rights, in support of the formal laws of slavery.[10]

Chapters 3 through 5 build on several cases introduced in chapter 1, explaining the impact of judicial discretion, changing legislative policies on manumission, and the significance of geography upon the litigation. These cases also bring to the fore notions of agency and narrative as developed in specific cases in which former enslaved women—alleged to have been the partners and children of slave owners—sued for inheritance rights. In chapter 1 I explain the broad strokes of narrative used by challengers to the wills and the judges in describing the men, but in later chapters I widen the focus to include how the men described themselves and how the women and children defined themselves in relation to the men.

Chapter 3 explains how the contest over Austin F. Hubbard's will had significance years later, after his daughter Narcissa was able to gain her freedom, inherit, and then pass on a legacy of freedom to her own children. This happened because judges on the Kentucky Court of Appeals supported manumission over slavery. Not only did Kentucky from its earliest history have policies that made it relatively easy for owners to petition for manumission through local courts, but the court supported manumission over enslavement. By the eve of the Civil War, the court continued this trend, notwithstanding the Kentucky legislature's tightened manumission requirements.

Chapter 4 returns to Mississippi and explores Nancy Wells's attempt to gain an inheritance from the estate of her late father. It explores tensions on the bench over the decision, explains why her effort failed in the courtroom, and demonstrates the significance of the legislature rejecting an earlier approach to manumission. The legislature heard petitions to manumit, and the legislators were previously willing to grant relief. But by the 1840s the standards an owner had to meet were onerous and unattainable for the average person: not all owners could demonstrate that slaves to be manumitted had performed some meritorious service to the state of Mississippi. Thus,

Nancy Wells's father, Edward Wells, used the legal strategy of removal to Ohio combined with a return to the home state and a bequest under his last will and testament.

Chapter 5 offers a contrast and considers in turn, Elijah Willis's successful use of manumission outside of the state combined with the careful use of a will drafted in Ohio that enabled the Supreme Court of South Carolina to support his partner Amy Willis's right to inherit. The South Carolina State Legislature once had in place a policy similar to Kentucky's, but it was rejected in favor of petitions to the legislature, a requirement more in line with Mississippi's system. This change resulted in a trend toward rejecting manumissions altogether; it fueled Willis's manumission strategy. The chapter also analyzes a unique community response, indicating the extent to which cases of contested wills could place whites into conflict over community mores, social control, and the community's interest in preventing miscegenation. White men in partnerships with enslaved women threatened upheaval of the social order and diverted resources from the white community. In a struggle against the court, local men petitioned the legislature to punish white men living openly with enslaved black women, but to no avail. The legislators refused to do anything.

This refusal indicates the limitations of popular control over issues of private property rights, interracial sex, and morality in the context of slavery. The legislators were unwilling to regulate white men's private behavior, regardless of the extent to which the men's behavior troubled the local populace. They might gossip and criticize, but they could do nothing to stop men so privileged by their class from doing whatever they wanted in their private lives, and that included the right to live in social equality with the enslaved women they owned. Nonetheless, as I expand on in the conclusion to this book, limitations could be imposed upon the men's death. Once the men died the enslaved women were unprotected. If the men made wills recognizing the women and children, they could be denied nonetheless; the men themselves could not automatically bestow rights to freedom and inheritance on their black slaves. But if the men had the foresight to use geography as a strategy in planning eventual manumission, the women and children could win in the end.

Understanding the rules of race, sex, gender and class in the antebellum South requires looking at the exceptions to those rules.

—JOSHUA D. ROTHMAN, *Notorious in the Neighborhood*

CHAPTER ONE

Righteous Fathers, Vulnerable Old Men, and Degraded Creatures

ROBERT WEISBERG HAS SUGGESTED that "narrative is a form of legal practice; legal practice and judging are partly ethical tasks."[1] Judges use their "skill in devising rhetoric to capture appropriate moral outcomes or to craft fair legal results . . . observing or crafting narrative patterns as a matter of situation-sense in conventional social settings where conventional moral issues may appear."[2] When state high court judges in the antebellum South used narrative to develop an image of the men whose last wills were contested, they built upon perceptions of ethics and morality in a slave regime. But these narratives did not question the morality of slavery altogether or consider the ways in which the law permitted only a narrow scope of tropes to choose from, insofar as agency could be held only by whites. The slaves at the heart of the contests were not testifying and developing narratives of their own.

What was fair? What was ethical? Did the legal system of slavery presuppose that bequests to slaves were improper, even when interracial sex was involved? Was it unethical for a slave owner to reject his legitimate white relatives in favor of an enslaved woman with whom he once engaged in immoral conduct? Might fairness entail upholding the wills, not only as a matter of protecting the wishes of the deceased, but as a matter of protecting the weak and powerless — enslaved women and children who had no independent legal rights? Because they were vulnerable to exploitation at the hands of slave owners and other whites in the community, should they gain rights to manumission and property?

In fact, the southern legal system presumed that black women were not vulnerable under the law. As Thomas Morris has noted, the "fullest protections" of sexual-offense laws "were reserved for white women with some social standing."[3] Manumission, in turn, "fell within the bounds of public policy even when it was seen in terms of private rights. The state had to give legal consequences to an emancipation, and emancipators had to comply with the rules or their efforts to release one from dominion would fail."[4]

In this chapter I explore the attitudes of southern antebellum jurists toward slavery, miscegenation, and the transfer of property from white men to enslaved black women, free women of color, and their mixed-race children, as found in antebellum will contests. I give a case-by-case analysis and categorization of the language judges used in describing the white men who left wills giving property to the women and their children: "righteous fathers," "vulnerable old men," and "degraded creatures."

The "Righteous Fathers" in the title of this chapter are those testators whose care for the women and children elicited at least judicial tolerance or neutrality, if not admiration and respect. These judges appeared to have an unusual view of mixed-race sexual relations in a slave regime. For these judges, white men providing for enslaved women and caring for their children was not unheard of, done quietly and discreetly. Thus the judges did not respond with rancor in determining whether the enslaved beneficiaries should receive under the will or keep the property they had been given. Their tolerance led them to fulfill testators' wishes and affirm the transfer of property, especially when precedents under the common law could easily be used to do so.

Born sometime in 1803, Nicholas Darnall grew up in Ann Arundel County, Maryland, the son of Bennett Darnall and an unnamed enslaved woman. In his will Bennett gave Nicholas several tracts of land, including Portland Manor, of 596 acres. Apparently there were two deeds of manumission executed by Bennett, purporting to free Nicholas and various other slaves. This case, which went all the way to the U.S. Supreme Court, *Le Grand v. Darnall* (U.S. 1829), did not lay in a suit for freedom.[5] Upon reaching adulthood Nicholas took control of the property, but the question was whether he had legitimate title to property he was seeking to sell in 1826. Referring to a Maryland statute, any owner wishing to manumit a slave could do so by will, but "no manumission by last will and testament shall be effectual to give freedom to any slave, unless the said slave shall be under the age of forty-five years, and able to work and gain a sufficient maintenance and livelihood at the time the freedom intended to be given shall take place."[6] Because the Maryland Court of Appeals had recently heard another case in which a three-year-old infant was denied freedom based on an inability for self-support, Darnall and the buyer of some of the property, Claudius F. Le Grand, decided to suspend the sale, especially when Bennett's heir at law "made claim to the land and threatened to commence suit for the recovery of it."[7] Le Grand and Darnall brought their case to determine Darnall's status and establish clear title. Darnall was eleven years old when his father died. Was he capable of taking care of himself at the time, or was he a slave at the time of his father's death?

The U.S. Supreme Court found the evidence to be in favor of Darnall. The rule with respect to manumitting those incapable of taking care of themselves did not apply in this case, according to Justice Gabriel Duvall, because four respectable witnesses from the community vouched for him: "Nicholas was well grown, healthy and intelligent, and of good bodily and mental capacity," fully capable of finding a job to support himself.[8] Moreover, Bennett had devised to Nicholas and his brother a considerable estate. The two young men demonstrated responsibility by having "guardians appointed"; they also "were well educated."[9] As a result, Darnall was affluent. Moreover, even if he were a slave at the time of his father's death, the fact that he was bequeathed property made him free by implication.[10] Thus, Justice Duvall ruled that Nicholas Darnall was fully capable of selling his property.

Various decisions from Virginia express in turn a liberal, matter-of-fact attitude taken by judges toward owner-slave sexual relations and grants of property to enslaved women and their children by the testators: though regrettable that white men had sex with enslaved women who then gave birth to mixed-race children, that was the nature of their society. One early case from 1809, *Bates v. Holman* (Va. 1809), grew out of a question of whether a will had been revoked.[11] When Charles Bates was a young man and single, he made up his first will. The year was 1799, and he left his estate to his parents and siblings. In 1803 Bates was still unmarried, but he had a slave daughter he mentioned in his second will, as noted by Justice Henry St. George Tucker: "having formed an imprudent (though not uncommon) temporary connection . . . he recognized the fruit of his unhappy amour, called his daughter Clemensa, declared her to be free, gave particular directions respecting her education, and made a handsome permanent provision for her, manifesting thereby a laudable instance of natural affection, and making the best atonement in his power, for his former indiscretion."[12]

Three years later Bates married. Thereafter, he cut off his signature from the second will and revoked the first one in a note onto the canceled second will. He kept both copies, however. By time he died in 1808, his father was dead and he had lately become concerned about providing adequately for his mother. He had mentioned to others that he had a will, the first one he wrote years before, but he wanted to change things. He didn't make the changes before his death, however, and did not mention provisions for his wife. They had no children. The issue before the court was whether he republished the first will when he said he still had it.

The court decided the case after a second hearing and argument.

The district court found in favor of the first will, but the judges of the Virginia Supreme Court were unwilling to support that position. Bates died without a will. He canceled the second one, and the court ruled that his statements that he had a will did not constitute republication of the revoked first will. Thus Clemensa did not receive the benefits laid out in the original will. Notwithstanding Clemensa's loss, one has the impression that had the second will not been revoked but had been challenged, the court might have been willing to let it stand.

About twenty years later was a case centering on the will of Francis Foster of Henrico County, who was the patriarch of a group of slaves, most of whom seemed to be connected to him through family ties, *Foster's Administrator v. Fosters* (Va., 1853). William Foster was Francis's son. The older Foster had children by one enslaved woman, Betsey Johnson: Martha Ann, Ellen, Eliza, and William Johnson, and children by other enslaved women. Wishing to free his children and their mothers, he brought them to New York City in 1831 for the express purpose of doing so. Included were William Foster and Betsey, Francis, and Thomas Johnson. He emancipated them by deed, having it witnessed and acknowledged by the mayor of New York. But when he died his executor seized them, claiming they belonged to the estate.

Justice Green B. Samuels, writing for the Virginia Supreme Court on the appeal of a court order granting their freedom, noted that "before going to New York, and whilst there, and after his return, [Foster] spoke of the trip to that place as intended for the sole purpose of giving freedom to the objects of his favor."[13] After Francis Foster manumitted them all, they returned to Virginia and "lived together as a family upon terms of equality."[14] Foster imagined that his manumission plan would circumvent the Virginia rule that made an application to the local court a prerequisite for manumission and permission to remain in the state. He later manumitted others of his slaves by a will dated 1835 and probated in 1836. None of those manumitted in 1831 were listed in his estate. They lived as free people for about twenty years, even though they had not been registered as free, until 1850, when they were taken into custody and claimed as slaves.

Neither Samuels nor any of the other judges commented on whether Foster was acting improperly in acknowledging his enslaved children and their mothers and in living with them as a family. There were no dissents and no other concurring opinions. The judges demonstrated a matter-of-fact acceptance of the lifestyle Foster chose. They refused to view his removal to New York as an illegal attempt to circumvent Virginia law; instead, he shopped for a forum and used a method that fulfilled his wishes, a perfectly legal and above-board strategy. He never intended that any of them would live as slaves ever again, and he treated them as such: "Thus there was nothing unlawful to prevent Foster from taking his slaves whithersoever he chose for any reason that to him seemed good: To hold otherwise would be an unjust interference with his rights to [relinquish] property."[15]

However, a few years later that right to dispose of property did not extend to free people of color inheriting slaves in the state of Virginia, according to *Dunlop & als. v. Harrison's Executors & als.* (Va., 1858). Nathaniel Harrison of Amelia County died unmarried in the summer of 1852. In his will he left three women of color a tract of land each: Frankey Miles, Ann Maria Jackson, and Laurena Anderson. Another tract went to the four youngest children of Edwin Harrison (probably Nathaniel's late brother), and each child received $100. Frankey Miles was to receive $600 a year as an annuity for life; Laurena and Ann Maria were to receive $250. He left the women all his household and kitchen furniture.

Harrison put contingencies in place for each of the beneficiaries "should they be required to leave the state." The beneficiaries were all free people of color because they were a population of people in the antebellum South who could be compelled to emigrate. He left them his entire estate. But in Justice George Hay Lee's view, the most controversial clause had to do with the residue of what was a substantial estate: twenty-five hundred acres of land, eighty-four slaves, stock, crops and perishables, and about eighteen thousand dollars in money and bonds. Harrison's executors were to become trustees of the estate for the support of Frankey, Laurena, and Ann Maria, and the children of the latter two, free from the debts and liabilities of their husbands. If his slaves had to be sold in order to create the trust, he wanted them to be sold to good owners in good homes.

The most controversial clause of the will was that by inheriting the entire estate, these free black women would gain ownership of slaves. Lee, in writing for the entire court, noted that under Virginia statutory law, "no free Negro shall be capable of acquiring (except by descent) any slave other than the husband, wife, parent or descendent of such free Negro."[16] Lee speculated that the purpose of the law was "to keep slaves as far as possible under the control of white men only, and prevent free Negroes from holding persons of their own race and color in personal subjection to themselves. Perhaps it also intended to evince the distinctive superiority of the white race."[17] Arguably, it also aided free blacks attempting to help their relatives still in slavery. Notwithstanding the proscription against ownership, the women could inherit because "it was never intended to forbid the free Negro to take the value of slaves in money or other property."[18] The court decided in light of the statute's parameters: the slaves could be sold and the proceeds set aside for the benefit of the women of color.

The legatees, Harrison's white next of kin, argued that with respect to the residue of the estate the women should inherit only what was necessary for their support. They hoped to limit the statement "maintenance and support" to mean only the bare minimum of what might be required. The judges did not agree and gave them everything: "the expression of a particular purpose for which the gift is made will not operate as a condition or limitation of the bequest."[19] They were more interested in fulfilling Harrison's general intent of giving the women the entire residue because:

> the most unbounded indulgence has been shown by the courts to the ignorance, unskillfulness and negligence of testators, and judges have even shown themselves astute in averting their effects. . . . [E]very allowance will be made for his want of better knowledge of the law as well as those of grammar and orthography. Where he may have obscured his meaning by conflicting expressions, his intention is to be sought rather in a rational and consistent than an irrational and inconsistent purpose. And if the will may admit of more than one construction that is to be preferred which will render it valid and effectual.[20]

With the exception of the bequests of slaves, the matters in contention seem uncontroversial. Missing was the vitriolic language found in other cases of this nature in which a white man left a substantial estate to people of color. Missing too was an explanation of the relationship Nathaniel Harrison had with Frankey Miles, Ann Maria Jackson, Laurena Anderson, and Edwin Harrison's children. But once again a similarity to other decisions can offer an explanation. Harrison was unmarried and had no known legitimate children. But he did have close enough connections with a group of women of color for whom he felt obliged to provide, to the exclusion of his white relatives, the collateral heirs who sued. These people of color might have been his family, known to everyone else, although it was not stated openly.

In *Greenlow v. Rawlings* (Tenn., 1842) there was no doubt of the nature of the relationship between the testator Isaac Rawlings and William Isaac Rawlings.[21] In February 1837 Isaac petitioned the Shelby County court to emancipate William, his son by a mulatto enslaved woman. Isaac always recognized him as his son, insofar as William was "brought up in his family as a free boy—and so regarded by the said Isaac, who never intended he should be a slave."[22] The chairman of the county court examined the petition and authorized it as being in accordance with the law. Isaac then gave bond so that William would never become a charge on the state if he ever became unable to support himself. After he died he made William executor and gave him his entire estate, all his real and personal property. The action before the court arose out of a note given by Thomas Rawlings to Isaac in July of 1837. William signed it over to J. O. Greenlow in May of 1841, but Thomas refused to pay, on the basis "that the endorser [William Isaac Rawlings], at the time of the endorsement and still, was a slave, and the endorsement void."[23]

The trial court judge instructed the jury that the record of evidence proved that William was free. His status could not be questioned, and the jury held for Greenlow. On Thomas Rawlings's appeal, Justice Nathan Green noted in his opinion for the court that although under statutory law a newly manumitted slave must leave the state as "part of the judgment of emancipation," an exception could be made in those cases where the contract for manumission was made prior to 1831.²⁴ There was no direct evidence establishing that fact in William's case; however, the court presumed it was found in the decree of emancipation signed by the court officer. The chairman of the county court had an opportunity to read the petition and examine the parties. Evidence of an agreement to free William could be found in what the court called "parol" evidence, the nature of the interactions between Isaac and William based on the presumption of an oral contract between them. It was obvious that a slave raised like a freeborn son in his father's house was only nominally a slave.

William Isaac Rawlings was lucky in that his route to manumission was a simple one: his father performed the manumission during his life, thus easing William's ability to inherit as the only beneficiary of his father's property. But others were not as lucky. Narcissa (or Narcisa), an enslaved woman and the reputed daughter of Austin F. Hubbard of Nelson County, Kentucky, was one of the unlucky ones. The county court admitted to probate a will in which Hubbard devised to her all his estate, provided her owner sell her freedom at a moderate and reasonable price. Apparently Hubbard had leased Narcissa and her mother from their owner, Dr. William Elliot, as house servants. If Narcissa did not become free, all went to Austin F. Hubbard Jr., the testator's illegitimate white son. Hubbard's white heirs claimed he was of unsound mind when he made the will. He was an alcoholic prone to drunken fits and delirium. But that alone did not mean he was incompetent to make a will, according to Justice Joseph R. Underwood in *Hubbard's Will* (Ky., 1831). The court found that Hubbard was sane and lucid when he made the will. He knew what he wanted to do and expressed his reasons for doing so: Narcissa was a faithful servant, she and her mother had been living in his house, and there were no other whites present. They were the ones he was closest to, because he was unmarried and had no legitimate children.

Hubbard had the will drawn by a draftsman. He then gave it to Narcissa for safe keeping, telling her that it was something important. Underwood applauded Hubbard's intent to provide for his daughter: "The obligation, in the nature of things, to protect and provide for illegitimate children, should be held as sacred as that to provide for legitimates. Indeed, it is the best civil atonement for the guilt of fornication."[25] The legal record does not state what had happened to sour Hubbard's relation with his son, so it is hard to know what to make of Underwood's finding that it was proper for Hubbard to provide for her, his illegitimate mixed-race daughter, over Austin Jr., "a son not tainted by African blood," because "of the faithful services of the one which he acknowledged, and the offensive conduct of the other, which had produced their separation."[26]

But that alone did not mean in the end that Narcissa won all she believed she was entitled to receive. Eleven years after the first litigation she was dead, and she still had not received the property. Her executors were pursuing the estate and litigation was pending, *Narcissa's Executors v. Wathan et al.* (Ky., 1842).[27] Peter Sweets had bought her half-brother's contingent interest in the estate in 1824 and might have been involved in the prosecution of the first case. He tried to buy Narcissa, but her owner refused unless it was for the purpose of freeing her. Sweets and the curator of the estate, Thomas Wathan, then signed an agreement with Elliot that they pay him $350 to emancipate her, if she would convey to them her entire interest in the testator's estate. Thus, in October 1831, seven months after the first case was decided, Narcissa became free. She signed over the estate, having been told by Sweets and Wathan that the estate was "insolvent."[28] But she was being swindled. Sweets thereafter filed a bill for division of the estate, claiming the personal estate was worth more than $10,000, and the real estate worth more than $5,000. By 1842, the date of the second lawsuit, about $1,400 of the personal estate was remaining and the real estate was worth $1,500.

Chief Justice George Robertson criticized Sweets for insinuating himself into the action for the purpose of stealing Narcissa's property and Wathan, who Robertson noted had a fiduciary duty "to disclose to Narcisa, frankly and explicitly, the situation of the [Hubbard] estate and her potential interest in it."[29] Instead, there was no "rational doubt that they made a fraudulent use of their peculiar knowledge and position, and unconscientiously deceived and imposed upon an isolated victim, who had not the ordinary means of rescue or resistance."[30] Equity demanded that the estate be audited and settled for the benefit of Narcissa's executors and trustees, to purchase and emancipate the children she gave birth to while she was a slave. One can make the argument that if Hubbard cared about his daughter so much he would have done all that he could for her while he was alive. Perhaps he could have bought her freedom, rather than hoping that her freedom would be bought after his death. Nonetheless, Robertson and the other members of the court of appeals did not hesitate to help her.

The court in Arkansas was just as helpful to another slave, a child who was three years old when her father died, *Campbell v. Campbell* (Ark, 1853). Duncan G. Campbell made a will in 1845, giving his estate to his brother and sisters, after "deducting therefrom five thousand dollars, which I bequeath to Viney, a yellow girl." One of his sisters was to take care of her until she turned fifteen, when she was to become free and receive her legacy. He had no lawful issue, and Viney was his only child.

Instead of being cared for by her father's relatives, Viney was sold in Missouri as a slave by Duncan's brother, Samuel Campbell, when he was acting as executor of the estate. He served from October 1845 until he was removed for breaches of trust in 1847. Another brother, Cornelius Campbell, took over as executor that July.[31] In January 1848 Samuel Campbell brought the suit that founded the basis of the action before the court. Other claimants included his sisters Mary and Flora Anne Campbell, against Cornelius Campbell, and other siblings. The purpose of the action was to declare "the bequest to Viney and so much of the will as purported to emancipate her were contrary to law and public policy, and void; and notwithstanding the will, Viney continued to be a slave and the property of the estate."[32] During the course of the trial, Samuel Campbell's misdeeds were discovered. The court declared Viney to be its ward and demanded that Samuel "produce her by the next term"; when Samuel didn't comply, the court found him in contempt.[33] The guardian appointed to represent her in the action was then charged with "ascertain[ing] where she was and reclaim[ing] her . . . by habeas corpus."[34]

Through Cornelius Campbell's accounting the court discovered that the estate was now not worth more than $5,000, due apparently to Samuel Campbell's removal of assets and to his waste of the estate. This was the amount of money Viney was supposed to receive, since it had been Duncan Campbell's intent "as he had often expressed during his lifetime, to liberate Viney."[35] She answered in turn, claiming that she was entitled to freedom and as much of the estate as would be required to provide her legacy. The lower court held in her favor, freeing her as per the will and finding that the legacy vested in her immediately upon Duncan Campbell's death. Cornelius Campbell then became her guardian. An appeal followed, and the Arkansas high court affirmed. Believing that her father wished to free Viney immediately upon his death, the court found Duncan Campbell's behavior reasonable: "Considering that Viney was the child of the testator, that she was of tender years, that it was necessary under our statute, for him to make some adequate provision for her support, to prevent her from becoming a charge on the public, at the same time confiding the care and custody of the child to one of his nearest relations . . . the will appears to be a sensible and judicious a one, albeit not technically framed, as any man in the unhappy condition of the testator, could well have made."[36] Nothing under Arkansas law barred him from freeing her, and indeed he followed the state policy of preventing free people of color from becoming wards of the state, by placing her under care and giving her a legacy worth more than the $500 bond a free person immigrating to the state was required to provide, in addition to a certificate of freedom, "conditioned for his good behavior, and to pay for his support, in case he should, at any time thereafter, be unable to support himself."[37]

The evidence as found in these cases indicates the extent to which the mixed-race children of white slave owners could reach a certain level of privilege. Their mixed-race status gave them access, not only through their fathers, but through their access to whites in the community who protected their interests. Although they were enslaved they were able to obtain freedom and property when their fathers embraced paternalism and other white men in the community— executors and judges hearing will contests upheld those paternal inclinations. They became upwardly mobile, occupying a class status different from other blacks who remained in bondage.

The "Vulnerable Old Men" are those testators who drafted wills that gave freedom and property to enslaved women and their children, but in these cases, the undue influence allegations of the challengers to the wills stuck, insofar as the judges hearing the cases found that the circumstances surrounding the legacy were suspicious. These were the vulnerable old men who lived in isolation from white relatives and friends, but who were apparently in the thrall of women of color who controlled them. These women forced them to act contrary to propriety's demands. The men thus did not leave money and property to their white relatives; instead, they gave everything to the women and their children. The courts stepped in and corrected the injustices, by holding for the legitimate heirs at law.

Davis v. Calvert (Md., 1833) is an example.[38] Thomas Cramphin of Montgomery County, Maryland, died at the age of ninety-two in December 1830. A month later Elizabeth Davis, his next of kin, filed an objection to the will filed for probate by the executor, George Calvert. She alleged George Calvert had colluded with Caroline Calvert, his daughter and former slave, to defraud Cramphin of his estate. The probate court directed the matter to the county court for trial, where Davis lost. She then filed an appeal over various jury charges and objections to evidence sustained by the county court.

Caroline Calvert became Cramphin's mistress when he was about seventy-five years old. During that time George Calvert was her owner. She received her freedom from him two days before the will was made in 1824, when Cramphin was eighty-five or eighty-six. Her deed of emancipation provided not only for her manumission but for the gradual emancipation of seven of her children. Those seven received bequests under the will. None of the others, the three born after her manumission, were to receive anything. She and the children were to inherit what Justice John Buchanan of the appellate court described as "a large estate."[39] George Calvert, the executor, was to take under the will if any of the bequests to Caroline and her children failed.

Caroline Calvert claimed that she had been Cramphin's mistress and companion for all the years she lived with him. She was a loyal and faithful servant. She took care of him and supervised his household. The children were his, and he recognized them as such. Davis countered that Caroline Calvert had been a prostitute the entire time she lived with Cramphin and that none of the children were his. Davis called witnesses whose testimony she claimed would prove that Calvert bamboozled Cramphin and exercised undue influence on a frail old man who was sterile. Other witnesses would testify that George Calvert, a few days after Cramphin's death, said that Cramphin "had promised . . . to provide for the children, yet that he did not consider himself bound to, because they were not [his]."[40] The trial court upheld the Calverts' objections to the evidence Davis proffered. Davis lost, but the appeals court reversed and remanded for a new trial.

Justice Buchanan was suspicious because of Cramphin's age and the drafting of a will that left everything to a newly manumitted slave and to some but not all of the children she allegedly had by the testator. It seemed that George Calvert, apparently a trusted friend of the testator, had helped perpetrate a fraud that had the potential to benefit him, since he could also recover under the will. The judges thus held that the evidence Davis proffered could be important for determining the circumstances of Cramphin's life and the making of the will. Caroline Calvert's character evidence was important. Thus, the court ruled that all was admissible.

At the remand, the nature of the evidence the court stated could be proffered might well have led to Elizabeth Davis winning the second time around. She could present many witnesses, presumably white men, who would testify that Caroline Davis was a prostitute, and in a society in which black women were deemed without virtue it is possible that they would have been seen as credible. Slaves in general could not testify, but because Caroline Calvert was no longer a slave at the time the action began in 1831, but a party to an action, she was capable of testifying, though she did not do so. One wonders whether she would have been believed.

But the woman alleged to have wielded the undue influence need not have colluded with others. In *Denton v. Franklin* (Ky. 1848) the relatives of Edmund Talbot, a white man debilitated by old age, alleged that a free black woman in his house had made him leave everything in his will to her, to the exclusion of his own children "whose condition and circumstances in life, required the exercise of his bounty in their favor, was entirely forgotten or disregarded."[41] Unfortunately, instead of being surrounded by people who cared about him, Talbot, as Justice James Simpson explained, seemed to have had no will of his own, but to have submitted implicitly to the dictation of a colored woman whom he had emancipated, and whose familiar intercourse with him had brought him into complete and continued subjection to her influence. The very fact that he undisguised yielded to an influence of such a character, and lost, under its exercise, apparently all independence of thought and action, leads irresistibly to the conclusion, that his mental faculties had given way.[42] Because Edmund Talbot was deemed not to have had the mental capacity to make a valid will, his will was rejected.

Also worthy of protection were those testators threatened by their legitimate white children for recognizing their illegitimate mixed-race offspring. Loyd Ford of Washington County, Tennessee, made a will in 1840 directing that John Ford and other slaves be emancipated and given real property. They were alleged to have been his illegitimate enslaved children. He named his legitimate sons, James and Grant Ford, as executors. They refused to serve, and the slaves brought an action by their friend Phebe Stewart to have the will probated. Some of the distributees and heirs at law then appeared and contested the will. The lower court found that the will was valid, and an appeal followed, *Ford v. Ford* (Tenn., 1846).

The opponents to the will alleged that Loyd Ford was of unsound mind, an elderly man with a failing memory. But notwithstanding Ford's advancing years, Justice Nathan Green, in writing for the court, found he was still capable of disposing of his property. The jury was entitled to hear and weigh evidence of his reputation and the nature of the relationship he had with the slaves. He had been heard to recognize them as his children, and the evidence corroborated it. There was no reason to believe he was insane. That he once told the keeper of the will to burn it, only to ask about it a few days later, did not prove insanity. Witnesses claimed that Ford complained that one of his legitimate sons "threatened to beat him, if he did not come and get the will. . . . Sarah Hale [Robert G. Hale's wife; she and her husband were both witnesses to the will] brought a paper which by the old man's direction was thrown into the fire. . . . The paper thrown into the fire was not the will."[43] Instead of being insane, Ford could have been wily, dissembling to avoid conflict with his son; the court recorded that "Some days afterwards the testator was at Hale's house, and enquired of Sarah Hale . . . if she had his will yet, she told him she had. He then said she must keep it, and do what he had before told her to do with it."[44]

Green thought that it was appropriate for evidence to be heard on the nature of the relationship between Ford and his mixed-race children. Such evidence would establish whether the old man was sane. Note, however, that notwithstanding this interpretation in the court opinion, one earlier commentator, Arthur F. Howington, has read the language of "children" to mean the paternalistic language of a slave owner for his figurative, but not literal, slave "children," thus removing from discussion the issue of how courts handled tensions within mixed-race families in which some were enslaved, others were not, and race divided them all.[45] In noting that the slaves had the right to bring their action, Justice Green set forth a liberal disquisition on the personhood of slaves:

> A slave is not in the condition of a horse or an ox. His liberty is restrained, it is true, and his owner controls his actions and claims his services. But he is made after the image of the Creator. He has mental capacities, and an immortal principle in his nature, that constitutes him equal to his owner, but for the accidental position in which fortune has placed him. The owner has acquired conventional rights to him, but the laws under which he is held as a slave, have not and cannot extinguish his high born nature, nor deprive him of any rights inherent in man.[46]

William E. Wiethoff notes, however, that apparent liberalism was not consistent; Justice Green also thought slaves were "unfortunate, degraded, and vicious."[47] Beyond that, free blacks were "an inferior caste in society, with whom public opinion has never permitted the white population to associate on terms of equality, and in relation to whom the laws have never allowed the enjoyment of equal rights."[48] This was the same Justice Green who held for William Isaac Rawlings.[49] Green's contradictions indicate that though he was not a consistent supporter of black rights, he did not seem troubled by the existence of Ford's mixed-race children. He might have been troubled, however, by adult children abusing their elderly father in an attempt to make him change his will. Finding Ford insane on the bare facts of a will leaving property to slaves, without any further inquiry, would have left open the door for the unscrupulous to take advantage of old men and deny them their personal freedom and autonomy.

In some jurisdictions in which judges frowned upon interracial liaisons, they nonetheless felt constrained to fulfill the testators' interests. These men were the "Degraded Creatures" who recognized their enslaved partners and their children. The will contests in these cases illuminate the extent to which these cases were battles over social control. White men who flouted society's mores by living openly with enslaved black women and recognizing their mixed-race children could not be controlled. But after their deaths their children and the children's mothers could be, insofar as these beneficiaries could be punished, not necessarily for the testators' illicit behavior but for the fathers' willful disregard of white familial and community interests in their wealth. Thus, the will contest was to some extent motivated by the interests of greedy ones seeking to usurp the men's prerogatives by maligning them.

This meant that claimants, for example the brothers and sisters of Ephraim Pool of Alabama, played on community prejudices and proposed legal presumptions that Pool was incapable of making a will, merely because the will was unorthodox. The proponents of the will would then have had the difficult burden of disproving the presumption of incapacity, and if the presumption stuck, the jury would have been forced to see the facts through its light, and the will could have been held invalid as a matter of law. Pool directed his executor George L. Stewart to take Harriet, described as a "mulatto woman," and several children she raised, to Ohio. The children apparently were Pool's by another enslaved woman. They were to be emancipated, his estate liquidated in its entirety, and all of the money invested on their behalf.[50] Harriet was to control the money.

So what did his siblings hope the jury would presume? They had several aims: that the will would be seen as unnatural and that it was written due solely to Harriet's inducement and influence. Theirs was an undue attachment, an adulterous connection, and his siblings righteously refused to associate with him as a result. Notwithstanding their disapproval, that should not bar them from receiving his property. They argued in *Pool's Heirs v. Pool's Executor* (Ala., 1859) that "he made his will out of spite" and "was acting under an insane delusion as to his brothers and sisters."[51] Moreover, Harriet might have induced the prejudice that caused him to leave her and the children all his property. But the presumption did not stick. The trial court did not permit it, and the high court reaffirmed.

Privileged by race and class, men like Pool lived their lives as they pleased and left their property as they saw fit, to the chagrin not only of their families but of judges critical of their behavior. As elite white men themselves, such judges could quarrel with the behavior, but the hallmark of liberty is a man doing with his property as he wishes. These battles sometimes amounted to fights within the courts themselves, among judges who were chagrined, and those who in various instances had been instrumental in helping men like these draft their wills. In the view of hardliners, these testators contributed to that anathema: a population of free blacks privileged by their intimate ties to white men.

W. B. Farr of South Carolina was sixty-six years old when he died in 1837. He made a will in 1836, adding a codicil in 1837. In the will he gave his entire estate, worth fifty to sixty thousand dollars, to W. P. Thompson, his executor. Farr had never married but according to the record "had lived for many years in a state of illicit intercourse with a mulatto woman, his own slave, who assumed the position of a wife, and controlled, at least, all the domestic arrangements of his family."[52] Her name was Fan, described as a "bright mulatto." She and Farr had one child, Henry, who was described as "nearly white." Years before Farr died he tried to free Henry by applying to the legislature, the only method of manumission available under statutory law, but that effort failed. Thus, when Henry came of age, his father sent him to Indiana, "where he had him settled, and provided him, from time to time, with considerable sums of money."[53]

The will in question was exactly like the one Judge John Belton O'Neall had written for Farr in 1828 when he was in private practice, prior to his joining the South Carolina Court of Appeals, except that in the earlier will O'Neall was named as executor. In each case Farr gave written instructions to the executor, declaring a trust relationship, explaining what should be done with the property: "execute for the benefit of Fan and Henry."[54] Those contesting the 1836 will were Farr's half-brothers, nephews, and nieces. Claiming the will was invalid due to the undue influence of Fan, they stood to inherit if the court found Farr died intestate. In their view Farr was under her control because she wielded the power of "a white woman and a wife."[55] He consulted with her and did what she said. Yet, they alleged, it was possible he was afraid of her, becoming more so as he got older. Hard drinking and "a stroke of the palsy" had debilitated him and impeded his ability to maintain his status as a slave owner.[56] They said Fan was also a drinker, and when she was under the influence she became particularly insolent, insulting and threatening him. According to one witness, Farr "did not know why he took up with [her]; when he was well and could go about, he did not mind her, but since he had been palsied, he had better be in hell."[57] The jury in the lower court found against the will.

By the time of the appeal O'Neall was on the high court and recused himself. Justice Baylis J. Earle delivered the opinion of the court, making an interesting comment on the undue influence allegation that was at the heart of so many of these types of will contests, *Farr v. Thompson, Executor of Farr* (S.C., 1839): "This phrase of *undue influence*, so frequently resorted to in this country, by disappointed relations, to avoid wills of persons on whom, while living, they had no claims, seems to me to be a modern innovation, and is not known in the English Courts" (original emphasis).[58] The litigation instituted by these claimants was deemed to have no basis. In Earle's view any reasonable and sane person could make a will, for the law permitted disposal of property at death, just as though the transfer took place while the person was alive. Thus, he explained: The testator was an intelligent man, of strong mind. . . . He had no lawful wife, nor children, and had not lived in amity, at least not in continued amity, with his relations; and he has given his property to a stranger to his blood. This he surely had a right to do, and this is all that appears on the face of the will.[59]

Notwithstanding Farr's long-term relationship with Fan, the social and legal culture did not accord her the status of a "relation," and if Fan had been his lawful wife, wielding the same level of influence, Earle noted that "it would not hold either with reason or law, to say that such an influence would avoid a will in behalf of the wife."[60] Fan was vulnerable only because she was an enslaved black woman. The undue influence alleged by the heirs at law did not hold, however, because the court took a narrow view of what coercion meant. The external threat or compulsion had to have existed at the exact moment when the will was written in 1836, and the court found none. As the earlier will indicated, Farr had intended since 1828 to provide for Fan and Henry. Yet the undue influence allegedly took place in 1835, before he made up the 1836 will. No matter how degrading the court found Farr's behavior, it was not unreasonable for Farr to provide for his son Henry, and to hold otherwise, as Earle wrote in his summary, "would be to let the jury run wild under the influence of prejudices and feelings which, however honorable and praiseworthy, must not be permitted to overthrow the rules of law, or divert the currents of justice. The trial by jury would otherwise become an engine of capricious injustice, instead of the safeguard of property."[61]

For this safeguarding of property was what the testators in each instance were trying to do: they endeavored to make provision for enslaved women and their children, under a legal system and social order hostile to such purpose. The culture of public opinion denied them, but they could try through arrangements with trusted friends and relatives charged with seeing the task through. Moreover, there were judges on the bench who were leery of politicizing the law in order to fulfill social demands. But nothing was more effective than making sure the manumissions took place before death.

This was what Elijah Willis did. In 1846 he made a will in South Carolina. An unmarried man of about fifty-three years of age, he left his property to members of his extended family, the heirs at law: his siblings and their children. Eight years later he went to Ohio and had another will drawn up by lawyers there. By this time his circumstances had changed; there were other people he wanted to make arrangements for, but he could not do what he wanted in South Carolina. He directed his executors to take Amy, his enslaved partner, her children, and her mother, to Cincinnati and emancipate them there. All his real and personal property in South Carolina was to be liquidated, with the proceeds going toward the purchase of land and the furnishing of a home for Amy and the children; they were also to receive the remainder of the money.

A year later in May 1855, Willis, Amy, her seven children, and her mother left South Carolina to set out for Ohio by train and then steamboat. But once they arrived, Willis died between the steamboat landing and "a hack he hired to take him to his lodgings."[62] The Ohio will was in his belongings; it was probated there on May 23, 1855, and the South Carolina will was probated when those back home learned of his death. Once the Ohio lawyers went to South Carolina to have the Ohio will probated, the heirs at law filed their bill opposing it, claiming insanity, fraud, and undue influence, alleging facts similar to those in the case of *Farr*.

Judge John Belton O'Neall heard the case at the trial level, and the jury found against the will. According to witnesses "the deceased was often under a gloomy depression of spirits — avoiding society on account of his connection with Amy, by whom he had several children; that he permitted her to act as mistress of his house."[63] She was demanding, outspoken, and an alcoholic. She might have been unfaithful yet was always careful to look out for herself and her children, at his expense. But another witness explained that Willis "was always anxious to secure the freedom of, and make provision for, Amy, and her children by him. . . . [I] never thought any of the matters . . . affected his intellect. I thought there was not the slightest ground to say that the testator was not of sane mind, or that there was fraud or undue influence."[64] The high court agreed in *Jolliffe v. Fanning* (S.C., 1856): "the will was made in Cincinnati in the absence of Amy, more than a year before the testator's death, a copy retained by him during the whole time."[65]

That Willis made a new will in Ohio appeared to vitiate any allegations of illegality under an act of 1841 that barred manumission in South Carolina. The sole question for the court was whether the will was valid. Willis freed Amy and the other eight and fulfilled the terms of the will. He "carried said slaves to Ohio in his lifetime, there left them, and there they remain, as far as we know."[66] It was in his right to do so, said Justice Thomas J. Withers. Contrary to being insane or under undue influence, Willis had made a careful manumission plan for Amy and her family. This was done of his own free will and reasonable mind. Willis conferred with Ohio lawyers because he would not have been able to find legal counsel in South Carolina to help him. Notwithstanding the "disgust" one might feel, Withers commented that men like Willis were to be pitied because "such motives and such provisions and such objects of bounty were perfectly consistent with the unconstrained pleasure and natural sentiments of such a man as Elijah Willis was."[67] His apparent moodiness and depression could be explained as such: "a sigh when he beheld the living examples of his shame . . . it is most obvious that the most rational his reflections and forecast, when he contemplated the channel through which he must hand down his blood to posterity, and the probable fortune of those who had sprung from him, the deeper must have been his gloom, the more bitter his remorse."[68] But such awareness of his misdeeds did not constitute insanity. The court ordered a new trial, and the verdict was in favor of the Ohio will.

The judges who developed the narratives of the men as found in these cases were presented with a limited set of tropes from which to choose. The culture of slavery presupposed an ideal of white masculinity. As Ariela Gross has explained, slave owners were supposed to be powerful, controlled, and invulnerable, experts in slave management.[69] But the men in these cases were essentially accused of not fulfilling that ideal. Their mastery was defective because they permitted themselves to fall under their slaves' control. Their addiction to drink robbed them of their senses, or their lust for black women made them foolish and careless. But some judges could find a counternarrative: that of a patriarch who took responsibility for his dependents, women and children to whom he owed specific moral obligations of care. What of cases where judges did not focus upon categorizing the men, but chose instead to consider the greater demands of the slave society? These cases, discussed in the next chapter, address the significance of judges' social policy arguments over miscegenation and inheritance rights.

Southerners turned to theology, history, political theory, law, science, and economics to defend the central institution of their society.

— PAUL FINKELMAN, "The Significance and Persistence of Proslavery Thought"

CHAPTER TWO

Slavery, Freedom, and the Rule of Law

CONSIDERING THAT LEGAL THINKERS of the antebellum South viewed slavery as fulfilling natural law and upholding the proper order of society, it is only logical that various judges hearing cases focused solely upon the formal laws of slavery.[1] They desired strict adherence to the law as established by local legislation and case law, in pursuit of the ultimate social policy goal: preventing an increase in the free black population. These judges were deeply suspicious of wills that appeared to manumit slaves within southern states and grant them privileges: property and status as free people. They denied manumission as a result.

But formal adherence to the law could be a two-edged sword.

Judges like O'Neall on the Supreme Court of South Carolina, who appeared to be less suspicious of testators' actions, could find in the wills requirements that fulfilled the demands of the formal law of slavery, for example, an owner charged with control over a slave, even though the slave was permitted to live freely. In these cases slaves were beneficiaries of a trust. Thus some slaves could gain a nominal free status. But that didn't mean they were fully protected. They had no rights to sue under the trust, and upon the trustee's death they were still property to be inherited.

Decisions from North Carolina indicate that the courts were called upon to adjudicate trusts set up for favored slaves, used when the law prohibited manumission in the state. The testators hoped to give the slaves the status of free people, even though they remained in bondage, a troubling concept to the appellate judges who heard the cases. Thomas Cunningham of Wilmington stated in his will that a Negro woman named Rachel would be given land and the rental incomes on various properties he owned, all for her benefit and "the maintenance and education of her three mulatto children, named Mary, Ritty and Chrissy, and the child of which she is now pregnant."[2] He desired that three other slaves, Virgil, Quash, and Tamer, remain on the plantation where he resided "to work for the maintenance of Rachel's children during the natural life of said negroes."[3] Finally, Rachel and her children were to become free immediately upon his decease.

Dr. Umstead of Orange County tried to do something similar in his will. He died in 1829, willing a Negro slave Dicey and her two children Emeline and Harriet to his friends Catlett Campbell and Thomas D. Bennehan. They were the executors, charged with undertaking "the necessary legal steps, to have said slave Dicey and her two children manumitted and liberated."[4] Until they were manumitted he wished no one to "benefit" from "the labour of such slaves, and the profits, and proceeds thereof."[5] A short time after Umstead's death, Campbell and Bennehan filed a petition for their emancipation: only Dicey became free. When Catlett Campbell died in 1845 his will asked that Bennehan remain true to the trust established by Dr. Umstead. He then relinquished any rights he had to the slaves, giving them to Bennehan. He didn't want the children or their descendants to become part of his estate; instead, he hoped they would gain their freedom through some other trust arrangement, provided it was necessary "to enable [Bennehan] to accomplish this purpose, if such release is necessary, or to sell, or convey them to any other person or persons, for a nominal price."[6]

In each case the North Carolina Supreme Court found the trusts were illegal. Slaves were not competent to take property, in the case of Cunningham's will, *Cunningham's Heirs v. Cunningham's Ex'rs* (N.C., 1801). According to Justice John Louis Taylor, "a civil incapacity results from the nature and condition of slavery. And it would be a solecism that the law should sanction or permit the acquisition of property by those, from whom it afterwards withholds that protection without which property is useless."[7] Beyond that, permitting a slave to live as a free person, as Dr. Umstead had planned for Dicey and the children, was illegal. The executors as residuary legatees received the slaves outright. Thus, the slaves Campbell owned who came from Dr. Umstead were considered part of his estate, liable for its debts, *Thomas D. Bennehan's Ex'qr v. John Norwood, Ex'qr & al.* (N.C., 1847).

Also in North Carolina, William S. Morris intended to manumit Patsy and her children Harriet, Albert, and Freeman. But the steps he took amounted to what the court found was an illegal attempt to free them and have them remain in the state. In 1831 Morris made up a will in which he gave Patsy and the children to his executor for the purpose of freeing them within a year of his death, using all money remaining in the estate "to effect the removal and emancipation as aforesaid" and to provide for their education, improvement, and subsistence.[8] Seven years later Morris added a codicil that devised them land, household effects, his cow and calf, and ten shares of stock in a local bank. Patsy was to use and occupy the property. After she died the children were to get it. Other pieces of land were to be sold for the benefit of William Henry Morris, Patsy's grandson by Harriet, who was to receive $1,000 out of the sale.

After William S. Morris died in 1848, his next of kin and various other legatees brought suit to void the emancipations and legacies to Patsy, her children, and grandchild. Significant to the court's opinion in the case was the fact that in 1828, Morris had brought them to Pennsylvania for the purpose of emancipating them, only to bring them back to North Carolina on his return, where they lived as free people. Judge William Gaston had previously advised him that the emancipation was irregular and might be declared void upon his death, thus advising Morris to make up the will. Gaston supported manumission as a matter of religious conviction; he served on the North Carolina Supreme Court from 1834 to 1844 but was not on the court when it decided the case.[9]

Upon Morris's death the executors tried to effect the slaves' freedom by taking them back to Pennsylvania with the intent that they would live there permanently. But the will held a contradiction. Judge Battle asked, how could Patsy and the others live in Pennsylvania when according to Morris they were to occupy and hold property in North Carolina? It was obvious that Morris intended North Carolina to be their place of residence, and the lower court thus held that the codicil of 1838 was contrary to state law and "the negroes Patsy, Harriet, Freeman and William Henry Morris, were still slaves, and belonged to the estate of the testator."[10] The supreme court agreed and dismissed a petition for a rehearing, affirming the decree of the lower court, *Green v. Lane* (N.C., 1852).

Lucy Thomas was far more successful at gaining her freedom. But due to a contradiction between the terms of the will and a codicil, she was not able to gain the property Nathiniel P. Thomas once left for her and her children Mary Jane, James, and Newton. Nathiniel intended that two plots of land in Caswell County, North Carolina, totaling 151 acres, be sold by his executors. They were to purchase a home for the family and place the remainder of the proceeds into an interest-bearing account. The interest on the remaining funds was to be used for their support, but before the sale took place the estate would provide funds for them to live on. In a codicil Thomas included a clause that he hoped would preserve the bequests to them in case North Carolina law "shall present an obstacle to the fulfillment of the trust."[11] The codicil directed that his "mulatto woman, Lucy, and her children" be removed to any "State, territory or country" that Lucy Thomas wished, and that funds from the estate be applied to pay for "their removal . . . and for their comfortable settlement there," since it was Thomas's "will and desire, that she shall not be continued in slavery."[12]

Once Lucy learned that she could not remain in North Carolina and receive the bequests under the will, she moved with the children to Ohio and became free. Ohio became their domicile. She then brought suit in North Carolina, explaining that through her own efforts and that of the executor, Nathaniel J. Palmer, they were able to get to Ohio, but she complained: "they have not been provided with a home or settlement as the will directs, and that they are in want, and destitution, and that the children being small, the mother is unable to provide for herself and them, without the assistance of the fund provided in the will."[13] She wanted the $1,500 proceeds from the sale of the properties and repayment for the expenses for her move to Ohio and the costs of their resettlement.

Palmer replied that, according to his advisors, nothing in the codicil validated what were "deficient and illegal devisees in the body of the will, so that the plaintiffs [were] not entitled to any thing but the expenses of their removal, and a comfortable settlement" in Ohio.[14] He already gave them the money to assist in their move and intended to provide for their comfortable settlement there, but he was waiting for the court's decision. Justice Richmond M. Pearson read the will and codicil in narrow terms, however, viewing the will first of all, as void, insofar as it would have elevated Lucy and her children to only nominal slave status, *Lucy Thomas and others v. Nathaniel J. Palmer* (N.C., 1854). They would have had special housing and funding for their support. Pearson ruled that to have permitted such a state of affairs would have fueled discontent among other slaves who knew them: "Free negroes constitute a distinct class; and the poor creatures seldom prosper so well as to become objects of envy."[15] Thus, all those becoming free were to leave the state, which was what Lucy did. But the codicil did not make valid the terms written in the will and did not authorize Lucy and her children to receive the fund provided by the sale of the land. Pearson thought the codicil was a substitute for the will, in case the will was held invalid. She could only receive from the estate the costs to cover her move and settlement in Ohio but would not receive income for the maintenance of her and her children.

Justice John Belton O'Neall in South Carolina was more open to such trust arrangements. Considering a case with a fact pattern almost identical to that in the case of Thomas Cunningham's will, he found instead that the assignment John Carmille made in 1830 of various slaves as part of a trust arrangement was proper, *Carmille v. Adm'r of Carmille et al.* (S.C., 1842). The trustees, George Pringle and Philip Chartrand, paid nominal consideration and received deeds for them. The contract permitted Henrietta and her five children, Charlotte, Francis, Nancy, John, and Elizabeth, to seek their own employment, work for their own maintenance, and exercise control over their earnings. They were to pay the trustees the sum of one dollar per year. Two other slaves, Tilly and Mary, were to apply their labor for the benefit of Henrietta and her children.

In 1832 Carmille had made a will in which he left his entire estate to Henrietta and her children, directing that they be manumitted within or outside of South Carolina, according to the law. That will was rejected, however, because apparently Carmille had been married in 1830 to Margaret Arnott, living with her for ten months before her death. Julia Carmille, claiming right as John and Margaret's legitimate daughter, was the complainant in the instant case. John Carmille died in 1833, and his daughter claimed that Henrietta and her children should be considered part of his estate: "the object of the bill is to set aside those deeds, and subject the slaves, in the first place, to the payment of the debts of the intestate, and to have the surplus paid or delivered to the complainant, as next of kin."[16] The lower court found the sale to be an "undisguised attempt to evade the law of this State, forbidding emancipation," and held it void.[17] An appeal then followed, and the high court reversed, with O'Neall writing for a unanimous court.

Significant to the case was whether the assignment to Pringle and Chartrand was designed to contravene the 1820 Act to Restrain the Emancipation of Slaves, which declared "that no slave shall hereafter be emancipated but by the Act of the Legislature."[18] But O'Neall did not see this case as violating any law: the slaves were not emancipated at all, insofar as they still had owners, and it did not matter that Pringle and Chartrand were to give them the fruits of their own labor: "Kindness to slaves, according to my judgment, is the true policy of slave owners, and its spirit should go . . . into the making of the law, and ought to be a ruling principle of its construction. Nothing

will more assuredly defeat our institution of slavery, than harsh legislation rigorously enforced."[19] O'Neall ruled that the purpose of the
contract was not to free Henrietta and her children but to ensure
that they would have kind owners upon Carmille's death.

Other evidence not presented at the trial explains exactly why
Carmille sought to create the trust. A petition he filed with the state
legislature in 1821 indicates that perhaps the lower court was right
about Carmille's intentions. He once tried to manumit Henrietta
and the children: "some years ago it was his fortune to form a domestic connection with a female named Henrietta & he has had by
her three children . . . according to the Laws of this state in the condition of absolute Slaves, the property of your petitioner."[20] He was
aware that he would be "open to censure as infringing the rules of
propriety and decorum," but he felt obligated to come forth because,
as he said in his petition, his family "who excluded as they are from
the blessing of Society, are still dear to Your Petitioner and dependent upon him for those comforts which the Policy of our Laws may
afford to that class of the community."[21] He would have manumitted
them before, but for the act of 1820 that established the legislature
as the sole body with authority to manumit. In answer to those who
would claim free blacks were incapable of self-support, Carmille explained in his petition to manumit that he had "a Sufficient Estate to
insure the comfortable maintenance of his said family, so that no ap-
prehensions can be intertained that they will ever become a charge
on the Public—That on the contrary his constant efforts [would] be
employed to support them decently & make them useful members
of society."[22] The legislature did not pass a petition of manumission;
as a result, Carmille sought the use of a trust.

In this case it appears the trust could stand because there was a
deed that conveyed ownership to another, and the slaves in question
could not sue to enforce the trust. Ownership having been transferred, the actions of the trustees were thus beyond the reach of the
claimants alleging illegality and improper possession of their testator's property. The testator gave up all claims to the slaves. Yet, under state law, the trustees could do what they wanted, for they were
owners in control of slaves. That meant in theory, they could violate
the trust arrangement, and the slaves would lose as a result, as in-

dicated in *Broughton v. Telfer* (S.C., 1851): "the beneficiaries being slaves could have no standing in Court to compel the execution of the trusts, which were thus of imperfect obligation, depending upon the benevolence of the trustee."[23]

So what good then was the use of a trust? Perhaps, as O'Neall suggested, it was meant only to ensure that favored slaves had good owners, but on the other hand, what if it could have been used for other reasons? What if the trustee, pursuant to the agreement with the former owner, permitted the slave to live as she pleased, to act as a free person, refusing to control her? What if the trustee then died, leaving beneficiaries to his own will who then claimed rights upon the slave? A trustee who acted as though ownership was in name only could sacrifice the inheritance rights of his own heirs, because his failure to assert ownership could be used by others to argue that the slaves were in fact free people, since he treated them as such. But what if the trustee was so lackadaisical about enforcing ownership rights that the slave was able to leave the state altogether and become free by moving to the North? Under all circumstances, the result was something to be feared by those concerned about the increasing numbers of free blacks in the community and their influence in the abolitionist North.

But in 1841 the South Carolina legislature put an end to the practice of creating trusts for the benefit of slaves. According to Justice David L. Wardlaw, "the policy of the State announced in the Act of 1841 . . . inhibiting the practical emancipation of slaves, and gifts and trusts for their benefit."[24] Thus, the trust William Hacket set up for the benefit of his slave Mary, their child Louisa, and her mother Alsey was found illegal. Hacket died in 1850, having drafted his will in 1847. In the fourth clause of the document, he gave the slaves to his brother Hugh, directing he settle them on a designated piece of land and build them a house. They were to receive all the profits of the land, interest income on $1,000, and the hire of another slave, Dick. They were to live as free people "without any person requiring or exacting any service or labor from them."[25] If any of the legatees to the will complained of the terms, the executors were directed to revoke the legacy of the complainant.

His sister Jane Mallet filed suit on the ground that the clauses for the benefit of Mary and her family were void under the law. Her brother Hugh responded that, in keeping with the terms of William's will, she forfeited the $2,000 she was to receive, as well as her interest in the residue of the estate. The court sided with her in *Mallet v. Smith* (S.C., 1852), ruling that the purpose of the clause was to terrorize. To permit it to stand would have meant that legitimate legal issues at stake would not be resolved. According to Justice Wardlaw, the act of 1841 established that those bequests as William made were "void as against public policy. . . . In the proper construction of the will, we must consider the fourth clause as struck out. . . . Besides, the legatees supposed to be disappointed here are slaves, who have no civil rights or *status* in Courts, through which they might assert a claim for compensation."[26]

That the formal rule of slavery presumed every black person a slave meant that a free person of color bringing suit could be accused of being a slave and therefore incapable of receiving a legacy. Thomas Hamilton of Davidson County, Tennessee, took out a $5,000 life insurance policy with the Mutual Protection Insurance Company on April 2, 1849. In August he wrote onto the policy that he was making the policy over to Adelaide Eliza Goram, a free woman of color from New Orleans. In February 1850 he was in New Orleans and had the endorsement witnessed onto the policy. Shortly after his death on August 25, 1855, Goram went to the insurance company's office to cash the policy. Andrew Hamilton, who became the executor of Thomas Hamilton's estate, also claimed the policy, arguing that because the estate might be insolvent, the money would be needed to pay the debts. The insurance company brought suit to determine who should receive the money. The case was heard by the Tennessee Supreme Court in Nashville, *Mutual Protection Insurance Co. v. Hamilton and Goram* (Tenn., 1857).[27]

Goram proved that Thomas Hamilton gave her the policy once he finalized the assignment, and that she had it since then. Andrew Hamilton responded that the assignment was not done pursuant to proper procedures, with notice to the insurance company. But more significantly, he did not believe that Goram was a free person "capable in law of taking any interest under the assignment."[28] Justice Robert J. McKinney, writing on behalf of the court, held that there was nothing in the insurance contract that required Thomas to inform the insurance company of what he had done. Moreover, once he made the assignment it had the effect of "divesting the assured of all interest in, and power of disposition over the policy."[29] Goram thus gained absolute rights to it. She had gone to the insurer's office, demanding payment, claiming her right as a free woman to do so, but the company's agent did not believe her. The court refused to permit Goram's status as a free woman to become an issue for litigation:

> These incidental allusions to the status of the defendant, were scarcely sufficient, perhaps, to have called for an answer, touching her social condition; much less to have put her upon proof in relation to it; yet she does answer as to this matter, and denying the right to raise any such question against her, she avers that she is a free woman, capable in law, of taking and holding property, and of suing and being sued. And there being no proof upon this point, the objection must of course fall.[30]

Adelaide Goram was a free person making a claim for an insurance policy, and her case was heard by a court that tended to be more liberal. But courts in Georgia and Mississippi usually focused more on the formal laws of slavery, particularly with respect to manumission taking place anywhere in the state. But when manumission took place elsewhere, the testators' intentions were more likely to be upheld. When Reuben B. Patterson clearly set forth that he entrusted George D. Blakely to become guardian to a three-year-old colored girl, Sophy, and remove her from the state of Georgia and free her, it was legal under Georgia law.[31] Sophy was the daughter of the enslaved woman Margaret. He did not want the little girl to be considered part of his estate. Instead, she was to be educated and remain in Blakely's care until she reached the age of sixteen, or until she married with his consent. She was to receive $2,000, the interest to be used for her education and support. If she were to marry, Blakely was to buy her a homestead. Blakely sued the executor, Alexander Cooper, in order to fulfill the terms of Patterson's will. Cooper claimed the terms were invalid and void as contravening the laws against the manumission of slaves. The lower court held for

Blakely, and Cooper appealed. Justice Warner replied that the will did not violate the law, *Cooper v. Blakely* (Ga., 1851).

Although Georgia had prohibitions against manumission in the state pursuant to statutes passed in 1801 and 1818, nothing prohibited manumission outside the state. Thus in several opinions Justice Joseph Lumpkin upheld various manumission plans, even though as he indicated in *Sanders v. Ward* (Ga., 1858) he had "no partiality for foreign any more than domestic manumission," but he did not see it as within his purview to "dictate to more than a half million of my fellow-citizens."[32] He just wanted all free blacks to stay away, and as for those about to become free, no slave should ever experience a moment of freedom in Georgia before gaining manumission.[33] The acts against manumission "were intended to prevent the emancipation of people of color in this state, where their presence could not fail to be injurious to the slave population . . . to the annoyance and injury of the owners of slaves."[34] Lumpkin's decisions revealed his thinking that such blacks were the allies of northern abolitionists, bent upon ending slavery throughout the South, a situation that only threatened to get worse as time went on and more slaves became free:

> Neither humanity, nor religion, nor common justice, requires of us to sanction or favor domestic emancipation; to give our slaves their liberty at the risk of losing our own. They are incapable of taking part with ourselves, in the exercise of self government. To set up a model empire for the world, God in His wisdom planted on this virgin soil, the best blood of the human family. To allow it to be contaminated, is to be recreant to the weighty and solemn trust committed to our hands.[35]

But with mixed-race individuals the danger was that they might pass for white and associate with whites on levels of social equality. As for the white men who had children by black and mixed-race enslaved women, they were contemptible. Commenting upon Joseph Nunez, the mixed-race child of a Portuguese man, James Nunez, Lumpkin noted, "he never learned to write his own name, and took up with negroes as his associates," instead of maintaining some level of society that he should have aspired to, as a man of some property.[36]

He married one of his slaves. But Joseph was only following the example of his father, who took a mulatto woman as his concubine. Yet as Lumpkin observed in his opinion, he styles himself a "gentleman." Men of this type were the ones who blurred the racial lines by trying to set their enslaved children free and providing them monetary legacies. Lumpkin wanted nothing to do with such men or their children: "which one of us has not narrowly escaped petting one of the pretty little mulattoes belonging to our neighbors as one of the family?"[37] But they were family in the eyes of the testators whose wills were at stake, regardless of whether the law or their communities agreed.

In cases in which legacies to children were at stake, the Mississippi Supreme Court, on the other hand, appeared the least willing to recognize the biological ties between testators and their children, and the desires those men might have had in keeping the children nearby and living with them. The formal language of slavery gave judges cover, particularly due to "the statute of Mississippi prohibiting owners of slaves to set them free without an act of the legislature (upon proof of meritorious or distinguished services rendered by such slave) approbating such act of emancipation."[38] These narrow prescriptions meant that the fathers of slaves could not free their children by deed or will. Fathers who sought to do so thus had to use their ingenuity.

As Paul Finkelman notes, this ingenuity led to tensions within the American legal culture over the issue of comity.[39] Northerners were tending to reject slavery once abolitionism held sway within their state jurisdictions. Southerners, on the other hand, by midcentury came to object to northerners' stance, one that they viewed with hostility and in absolute rejection of the ancient Constitutional compromises. Should southern jurisdictions recognize the rights and interests of free people of color? Eventually, the answer, in Mississippi, at least, became an unqualified "no." As long as northerners recognized former slaves as free people of color, they harmed southern interests in maintaining slavery in their jurisdictions.

Elisha Brazealle took his son John Monroe and his son's mother to Ohio in 1826, where he gave them deeds of manumission. They then returned to Mississippi, where they lived until Elisha's death. As reported in *Hinds v. Brazealle* (Miss., 1838), in his will Brazealle "recited the fact that such a deed had been executed, and declared his intention to ratify it, and devised his property to the said John Monroe, acknowledging him to be his son."[40] Bringing suit were Elisha's heirs at law. But Chief Justice William L. Sharkey, in writing for the court, refused to affirm the trial court's judgment in favor of John Monroe. The emancipation was ruled void because "no state is bound to recognize or enforce a contract made elsewhere, which would injure the state or its citizens."[41] In freeing his family, recognizing them and giving his son property, Brazealle contravened the social policy against increasing the local free negro population, and undoubtedly violated norms against racial mixing: "the contract had its origin in an offense against morality, pernicious and detestable as an example. But above all . . . planned and executed with a fixed design to evade the laws of this state."[42]

But Jonathan Carter of Mississippi wanted to go further by sending his mixed-race daughter into the white world, where she might pass for white. He conveyed to Joseph Barksdale "a yellow girl, nearly white, named Harriet, aged twelve years, born of the house-woman Fanny."[43] Barksdale was to raise her as white. Carter instructed that she not be treated as a slave; she was to enjoy the fruits of her own labor and live in Barksdale's household. She could complain to her guardians, B. B. Wilkes and his wife Elizabeth, if she was being mistreated. If she married a free white man, Barksdale and her guardians were authorized to set aside property for the benefit of her and her children. Those terms, granting her nominal slave status, in the eyes of Justice Ephraim S. Fisher, didn't mean the deed of sale was void, *Barksdale v. Elam* (Miss., 1856). Instead, the illegal conditions were "contrary to the spirit and policy of our laws."[44] Barksdale owned her outright and was not obligated to fulfill the terms stated in the will, as a matter of law; that meant Harriet had no recourse if the terms of the will were not fulfilled.

One means available to testators wishing to free their children and give them property entailed sending them out of state, never to return. Thus, James Brown took Harriet, a mulatto woman who was his slave, and their two children, Francis and Jerome, to Ohio. He gave them deeds of manumission and then took them to Indiana, where he owned property. He sent the children to school. They lived there with their mother and did not return to Mississippi; instead, Brown visited them, dying there in 1856. Described by Justice Alexander Handy in *Shaw v. Brown* (Miss., 1858) as "infatuated or debased," he nonetheless made an effective devise of his property. All his property and slaves in Mississippi were to be liquidated, "and after paying the debts of the testator . . . deposit the surplus in the Bank of Louisiana, subject to the order of Francis M. Brown, and in the case of his death, subject to the order of Jerome M. Brown."[45]

Neither his sons nor their mother could hold property in their home state of Mississippi because it was illegal for free blacks to remain in the state or immigrate to the state, insofar as "the mischief intended to be prevented, was their improper interference with our slaves, or the force of their example, in producing discontent and insubordination among them."[46] What is significant, however, was the language used to define them, young men who had been born and raised in Mississippi, the children and heirs of a white male resident. Freed by their father and living in the North, they were in the eyes of the heirs at law, similar to "alien enemies, outlaws, or banished persons, and are excluded from all protections of our laws, and from all rights here."[47] Justice Handy did not agree with that harsh assessment, however. All the evils stemming from their status as free blacks were eviscerated by the fact that they did not have to come into the state to receive their legacies. Richard D. Shaw, the executor, was charged with conducting the sale. The money was going directly to a bank in Louisiana.

However, that scheme for leaving property did not last long. One year later the Mississippi Supreme Court decided *Mitchell v. Wells* (Miss., 1859), a case with facts similar to those in *Shaw*, but the court refused to uphold this time around. Nancy Wells was the daughter of her slave owner Edward Wells, who died in 1848. She alleged that her father freed her by taking her to Ohio in 1846 and settling her there. When he died he gave her a legacy of a watch, a bed, and $3,000. Since she was still a minor, he charged the executor to manage the property. The executors resolved the estate and divided the property, but William Mitchell, an executor, held onto the money when it was rightfully hers, according to her allegations: "the defendant retains the legacy on the pretext that the complainant is a slave," but her father "recognized and treated her as a free woman" as did the laws of Ohio.[48] Mitchell replied that Nancy Wells was still a slave because any manumission had been fraudulent: "the testator took complainant to Ohio in fraud of the laws of Mississippi, and with the intent to return to this State."[49] In his view she never really lived in Ohio, since she returned to Mississippi only eighteen months after she left.

Justice William L. Harris, in writing for the court, focused not on the reasons that Edward Wells would have given Nancy Wells the bequest, or on whether she truly was a resident of Ohio. Instead, his sole concern was on what her freedom and access to property might mean to Mississippi: "on the subject of African slavery, we find this race in this inferior, subordinate, subjugated condition, at the time of the adoption of the Federal Constitution . . . unfit by their nature and constitution to become citizens and equal associates with the white race in this family of States."[50] Because slavery was essential to the social, political, and cultural well-being of whites in Mississippi, he deemed that the state "had a right to full protection . . . both for the enjoyment of her property in slaves, and against the degradation of political companionship, association, and equality with them in the future."[51] The Mississippi judge did not talk about the father-child relationship, hiding behind the formal laws of slavery to deny paternalism.

The popular understanding of Louisiana slave society has described it as a more liberal one, in which interracialism was more fluid. Mixed-race liaisons were more common and tolerated, leading to a population of free people of color who occupied a middle ground between white and black. The formal laws of slavery did not apply in the same way it did in the common-law jurisdictions because manumission was easier and free blacks could live within the state. The white community was not as concerned about an increasing number of free blacks with access to wealth and ties to the white elite. White men's liaisons with free women of color were seen then as matters of personal preferences and morality. Notwithstanding that popular view, that did not mean that there was no color bias, and that did not mean that the formal laws of slavery did not apply when inheritance rights were at stake and enslaved women or free women of color sought to inherit from slave owner partners and fathers. They might enjoy his support during his lifetime, but upon his death the formal law of slavery could deny them rights to inherit.

The French counsel at New Orleans explained to Alexis de Tocqueville in 1832 that the nature of Louisiana's slave society contributed to "great immorality" among the colored population, for "the law in some sort destines women of colour to wantonness."[52] Even though some were so light skinned as to appear to be white, they were barred from full participation in white society. Even if they were educated and cultured, the one-drop rule applied, insofar as "tradition [made] it known there [was] African blood in their veins."[53] In this caste society, darker-skinned people of African descent, regardless of their status as slaves or free people of color, were divided from lighter-skinned blacks, especially when the lighter-skinned blacks were free. These lighter-skinned blacks were more like whites, but they were not really white. Neither were they fully black. Women of this group could not intermarry with whites, and marrying a man of color was not advantageous, "for men of colour do not even enjoy the shameful privileges that are accorded their women."[54] Among these privileges were undoubtedly the access they had to wealth through white male protectors.

The quadroon ball, long notorious in New Orleans society, was the "link produced by immorality between the two races," where "coloured women destined in a way by the law to concubinage."[55] The romanticized view explains that free black women, often of mixed race, went to the balls in search of white men willing to become their partners to provide them residences and money for their support. Living in a society where their access to wealth was proscribed, concubinage could be a means of becoming upwardly mobile, as the men supported them, paying for their upkeep and taking care of any children they had. These women had status as free women who ran households and owned slaves. But how were they treated under the law? What was the effect of being barred from the status of wife?

During the course of their relationship, they were free to live as they pleased, and they could be treated as partners. Thus, a free woman of color living with a white man who permitted him to receive her negroes' hire without calling him into account, was presumed to have allowed the hire as part of their joint expenses, as indicated by *Tonnelier v. Maurin's Ex'r* (La., 1812).[56] But if things went awry, free women of color were not as well protected as white wives. So when Achille B. Courcelle ended his relationship with Louise A. Vitry after having lived with her for nineteen years, he successfully sued for the property in real estate and slaves that he claimed he bought with his own money but put title in her name, *Courcelle's Syndic v. Vitry (f.w.c.)* (La. 1860).[57]

It appears that because these women had free status, they had room to negotiate the bases of their relationships. Will contests before the courts raised the question whether white men and the black women they were involved with were lifetime partners or whether the women were in fact concubines. These were free women, able to sue. But what could they sue for? What could they expect to gain? If a woman alleged that she and the man lived together as lifetime partners, notwithstanding the lack of marriage, she could lay a claim for part of his estate: in "the universal partnership all goods and effects, both present and future, [became] immediately the joint property of both of the contracting parties," according to *Bore's Ex'r v. Quierry's Ex'r* (La., 1816).[58] But the concubine, seen as nothing more than a servant, "whose union was an immoral one," had no cause of action to sue for his entire estate.[59] She could inherit only "a donation of moveables limited to one-tenth part of the whole value of the testator's estate," as was stated in *Compton v. Prescott* (La., 1845).[60] Movables amounted to personal property, not land and houses.

Any executor or heir could thus sue for property alleged to have been given by a white testator to his concubine, including notes amounting to $123,451.50 given by Hart to Boni, the free woman of color with whom he lived prior to his death. This was the amount in notes that Boni had in her possession when Hart died. His executors, charged with "powers to take possession and inventory," were thus "authorized to bring an action to recover any property which may have belonged to the testator at his death."[61] Because she had no legitimate status she could be dispossessed, as ruled in *Executors of Hart v. Boni (f.w.c.)* (1833).

Women like Anna Sinnet could also be evicted from the houses they lived in. Sinnet had lived with Joseph Uzee in concubinage, prior to his marriage. She bought a slave for $700 cash, and in 1841 Uzee sold her a house for $3,500. The court found the purchases to be made with his money, because "the fact of concubinage and the absolute inability of Anna Sinnet to pay the price mentioned in the acts of sale . . . and the evidence in the record satisfactorily shows those sales to have been disguised donations," *Dupre v. Uzee* (La., 1851).[62] On the other hand, in a case in which Gregorio Bergel conveyed all his property to Mary Bergel, a free woman of color who had once been his slave but who later became his partner, the claimant creditors, alleging the sale fraudulent, were obliged to prove that the conveyance had been done in contemplation of his debt, for the sole purpose of evading payment. In the eyes of the supreme court of Louisiana, Bergel was not scheming, *Lopez's Heirs v. Mary Bergel (f.w.c.)* (La., 1838). The court came to this conclusion because "the sale was in January, 1833, and the judgment was not rendered against Bergel until January, 1834 . . . [the notes,] due in August 1826 . . . which, apparently, had been prescribed by a lapse of five years."[63] Nonetheless, at stake were not just the interests of the debtors, but those of the heirs at law. As a result, the court remanded.

Lawsuits such as these could also be a means of claiming money belonging to free black women of independent means, just because they were involved with white men. Eugene Macarty began in 1796 what was to become a long-term relationship with a free woman of color that lasted until his death in the 1840s. It was "the nearest approach to marriage which the law recognized, and in the days in which their union commenced it imposed serious moral obligations. It received the consent of her family, which was one of the most distinguished in Louisiana."[64] She belonged to the Mandeville family, but her first name was not given. Was she part of a distinguished free family of color? Was she descended from a prominent white family? It is unclear. But what was clear, however, was that she was "une femme extremement laborieuse and econome": an extremely hardworking and economical woman. An excellent businesswoman, she had made a fortune selling dry goods and was worth more than $155,000, of which $111,200 was banked in her name. By Macarty she had five children, of whom four survived. All were well educated. Two sons were in business, and one lived on his income. A daughter was married and lived in Cuba.

When Macarty died his relatives claimed that the money was all his, that he had given it to her in contravention of the law limiting the inheritance rights of concubines. The action failed, however, *Macarty v. Mandeville* (La., 1848). Plenty of witnesses testified to her business acumen. She bought goods and property, selling them and making a hefty profit over a lifetime of industry. If anything, Macarty's money went toward a failing plantation in Cuba as well as toward "the expenses of his own household, and of the education and establishment of his own children," as court testimony noted.[65] Notwithstanding the evidence presented before the trial court that proved Mandeville's wealth was independent from her partner's, the plaintiffs made appeals to race and slave culture that Justice George Eustis felt compelled to answer:

> We are not insensible to the appeal made to us in this case, in the interest of morals, religion and social order. . . . we have . . . reversed the verdict of a jury, vindicating the rights of heirs and restored to them a large estate, which a party had attempted to deprive them by an indirect donation to a concubine. . . . At the same time that we are bound to give effect to our laws made in the interest of families, it would be an abuse to bring them into conflict with the right of property.[66]

The social order demanded that the law protect the property interests of white relatives, heirs over concubines not seen as life partners. It was what moral and religious sentiments demanded. But in the instant case, Mandeville's obvious property interests mattered more, because there was no basis to the claim that her wealth was not hers. Prejudice was the sole motivator, and the court was unwilling to let such sentiments hold sway. Nonetheless, in will contests like these, judges still felt obliged to protect white relatives and the pureness of the white race. According to Justice Isaac T. Preston in *Badillo v. Tio* (La., 1851): "there exists in our State a public policy, perhaps an absolute necessity, to discourage the amalgamation of the white and colored race. . . . Here, marriage between the two races is forbidden by law; the honor of marriage shall not be debased by the connection."[67]

Although free women of color experienced disabilities under the law, enslaved women suffered more. Not only could they be owned by more privileged free women of color, but if they were freed by a will, the manumission could be denied if they were found to have been concubines. The rule that limited the inheritance rights of free women of color was thus extended to enslaved women. A bequest of manumission could be offset depending on whether the enslaved woman's worth was more than what the law said the heirs should inherit. Moreover, the enslaved woman's status provided no legal excuse for her concubinage, according to Justice Preston. A female slave named Jane was owned by Henry C. Vail; he freed her in his will and gave her two promissory notes worth a total of $200. His lawful heirs challenged the manumission and inheritance because she was a concubine, but the executor, Bird, objected "because the slave was entirely subject to the power of her owner and without a will of her own."[68] The lower court agreed with Bird and dismissed the plaintiffs' suit. They appealed. Preston, writing for the high court, disagreed and reversed, *Vail v. Bird* (La., 1851). He found that under the law Jane was protected: "the slave is undoubtedly subject to the power of his owner; but that means a lawful power, such as is consistent with good morals. The laws do not subject the female slave to an involuntary and illicit connexion with her owner, but would protect her against that misfortune."[69]

It is unclear how the law protected her. Thomas R. Cobb, a southerner and a lawyer, writing on the slavery question, discussed just what rights slaves had in this period: "Of the three great absolute rights guaranteed to every citizen by the common law, viz., the right of personal security, the right of personal liberty, and the right of private property, the slave, in a state of absolute slavery, is totally deprived, being, as to life, liberty, and property, under the absolute and uncontrolled dominion of his owner."[70] In Cobb's view the rape of a female slave by her owner was "almost unheard of; and the known lasciviousness of the negro, [rendered] the possibility of its occurrence very remote."[71]

Barred from testifying in her own offense and under the absolute dominion of the man who owned her, the female slave could not bring a lawsuit except for her freedom. She could not file a complaint before the criminal courts that her owner sexually assaulted her. If she had children by him, he was under no obligation to free her or them. If anything, the law enforced her subservience and made her vulnerable to exploitation. Nonetheless, Cobb found that "the female slave is peculiarly exposed, from her condition, to the seductions of an unprincipled owner. That is a misfortune; but it is so rare in the case of concubinage that the seduction and temptation are not mutual that exceptions to a general rule cannot be founded upon it."[72] An enslaved woman thus had, in his opinion, a certain level of agency to negotiate a consensual sexual relationship with her white male owner and become a concubine. But the contradiction was that such relationships, if they existed, could be used by the law to deny her the freedom and property the testator meant for her to have.

Thus, Sukey Wormley's lack of a sexual relationship with her owner preserved her in the eyes of the court. The heirs of M. C. Hardesty "sought to reduce her to slavery, and to deprive her of all her property, upon the alleged grounds that she was the public concubine of Hardesty."[73] They lost at the trial court and appealed. Thomas Slidell, writing for the court in *Hardesty v. Wormley* (La. 1855), found that "the evidence admitted at the trial [did] not prove it."[74] In 1834 Hardesty petitioned to free her and her daughter Adeline. When he bought them from Wright, her former owner, she gave money toward the purchase of their freedom. The agreement between Hardesty and Wright was that "Hardesty would emancipate her and her child as soon as she should refund the money advanced."[75] And that is what she did: "by unusual industry, economy, and good character, she afterwards made a great deal of money, laboring day and night for the purpose of purchasing her offspring; that she has paid for herself and them, and that what she now has is the fruit of her honest and persevering exertions during a long course of years, in a community where she seems to have enjoyed general confidence and respect."[76] Apparently Justice Slidell was willing to free her even if she had been in concubinage with Hardesty. What mattered more was the agreement between the two white men who once owned her:

"the fulfillment of his promise of emancipation—a lawful promise, which his obligation to the vendor bound him to fulfill, and which legally enured to the benefit of the slave."[77]

Even if a slave had some level of agency and could persuade her owner to free her, the inheritance laws limited his ability to do so, because under Louisiana law heirs were entitled to a guaranteed portion of a testator's estate. Thus, even though William Adams Jr. freed his slave Nancy in his will, providing her money, a watch, and his furniture, his father successfully sued to have the bequest overruled, since heirs at law were obligated to receive a specific portion of their benefactor's estate. Thus the father was "the forced heir of the one undivided fourth of his son's estate," *Adams v. Routh and Dorsey* (La., 1853), and any bequest of emancipation had to take into consideration that requirement.[78] Otherwise, the standard was that the emancipation could be viewed as a "fraud" upon the white heirs, according to *Virginia and Celesie, f.p.c., v. D. and C. Himel* (La., 1855).[79] Giving Nancy her freedom amounted to giving her a sum of money in the value of her own worth, but since her worth was greater than the amount available for each heir, the bequest failed. The estate's value, including her, was worth $4,750, and she was worth $1,000, or about 21 percent of the estate. In the eyes of the court the bequest of her freedom was thus "excessive." As for "two bastard children of the testator" who received legacies of $1,000 each under the will, they were to get their share after their grandfather received his.[80]

It is unclear whether these two children were Nancy's. If they were, the court elevated them above her, to take their legacies, while hers was denied. Because the court authorized partition, a division of the property between all those receiving bequests, she could be sold for their benefit. She was the sacrifice, for the benefit of the testator's father and for the benefit of children who could have been her own. But enslaved women were sacrificed under the law in many respects: their bodily autonomy was not respected, and they were valued only for their labor and the children they produced. Their children, born of liaisons with white men, could escape enslavement and receive property from their fathers.

Those freeborn children could be acknowledged, even though they were illegitimate, provided their fathers did so "in the registry of the birth or baptism, or by a declaration before a notary public, in [the] presence of two witnesses," according to *Pigeau v. Duvenay* (La., 1816).[81] Proof of paternity was not enough, but the formal steps had to be pursued. If their fathers were married, however, they sustained further disabilities, because "bastards, adulterous or incestuous, even duly acknowledged, [did] not enjoy the right of inheritance," as indicated by *Jung v. Doriocourt* (La., 1831).[82] But white illegitimate children (not of adulterous or incestuous unions) could prove their paternal descent, even if they had "not been legally acknowledged, provided they be free and white."[83] This proscription was necessary, because in the opinion of Justice François-Xavier Martin, a native of France who received his earliest education in a Jesuit academy, the new world of Louisiana called for new legal rules: "cases of bastardy, of very rare occurrence in France, [were] unfortunately, much more frequent among us. . . . these [were] very important considerations which [imposed] on our courts a stricter observance of the laws relating to illegitimate children, especially those of color."[84]

These laws placed the mixed-race children of white fathers at a disadvantage to white illegitimates when it came to claiming inheritances from them. Even if their fathers made provisions for their mixed-race children to inherit, they could do so only if the men were unmarried at the time of their birth and had already gone through the process of acknowledgment; if the men took none of these steps, the children had no recourse. On the other hand, white illegitimate children could inherit whether the white father had formally acknowledged them or not. In a society in which free black women were deemed concubines and barred from marrying their partners, their children lacked equal protections under the law. It was thus easier for their children to be disinherited, and more difficult for them to claim their status.

Such a policy operated to protect testators' estates, as Justice Pierre A. Rost, a landowner and industrialist, explained in *Badillo v. Tio* (La., 1851): "if colored children might make proof of their paternal descent from a white father, they might receive by testamentary dispositions, portions of the father's estate, and without a will, claim alimony from his legal heirs, thus giving direct encouragement to the degrading evils which the exclusion of the proof by law was intended to remedy."[85] But "where the parent has been so lost to shame as to make an authentic act of his degradation" and the formal steps had thus been pursued, a mixed-race child could inherit.[86] But that inheritance was only limited to a quarter of the estate, because if a testator died without legitimate descendants, he was forced to give a portion of the estate to his legitimate relations, the collateral heirs: brothers, sisters, nieces, and nephews, among other relatives, according to precedents established by *Prevost v. Martel* (La., 1845) and *Compton v. Prescott* (La., 1845).[87]

Important, too, was protection of marriage, the foundation of white society, Rost noted:

> Here, marriage between the two races is forbidden by law; the honor of marriage shall not be debased by the connection. Moreover, the inestimable advantages of marriage to society, shall not be disregarded by encouraging illicit and debasing concubinage with the colored race. . . . Recognizing the rights of mixed race colored children to claim a share of their fathers estate would fly in the face of the public policy and "diminish the father's estate to the prejudice of his white and lawful heirs.[88]

To permit marriage between whites and blacks would mean the end of white society by creating an amalgamated race that so troubled Lumpkin of Georgia, and would bring about the end of slavery itself as enslaved women achieved legal and social equality with white women through their relations with white male husbands eligible to free their wives. It would also spell the destruction of the South's wealth in slave property as their mixed-race children gained status as the legitimate children of their fathers. This parade of horrible possibilities was to be avoided at all costs. In the case of white fathers of enslaved children, all legal channels to effect this social and legal equality were to be barred and their prerogatives as white men usurped, to their shame, in the name of the greater social good: white supremacy.

Shaming testators who fathered mixed-race children by enslaved women and free women of color and sought to fulfill their paternal obligations to those women was thus the ultimate goal of certain legislators and judges. Even though the testators were dead, their cases could be used as examples to other men of how elite white men, the judicial arbiters of society's rules, saw them. They were free to live their lives as they wanted, and mixed-race intimacy was so common in Louisiana as not to be unusual. But bequeathing blacks and mixed-race children valuable property, their freedom, and a foundation of wealth was beyond the pale for those elite jurists, who were sympathetic to white relatives suing to overturn the will. Testators' status as white men did not save them in this struggle over white supremacy and property.

The formal law of slavery could be used as a weapon, and judges in Louisiana were more than willing to use it. It was only when the facts of the case were obviously indicative of a formerly enslaved woman's lack of sexual connection to her owner or of a free black woman's financial independence that the women could defend their right to freedom or their right to keep their own money. Under those circumstances the judges felt constrained even though they realized that the greater social demands of the community wanted them to hold otherwise. But what happened in a jurisdiction where the formal law of slavery truly was more liberal, insofar as the state's early laws established manumission requirements favorable to owners seeking to liberate their slaves? How did that affect judges hearing cases of contested wills where miscegenation was alleged? How did the judges then respond to tightening manumission practices that developed over time as the conflicts over abolition began raging?

The next chapter turns to Kentucky, reintroducing the case of Austin Hubbard and considering the decision in light of Kentucky's history as a state adjacent to the North—the free state of Ohio shared Kentucky's border on the Mississippi River. Kentucky had large populations in the community that were not as reliant upon slavery, thus giving greater voice to the antislavery cause. Chapter 3 then considers later cases that demonstrate an increasing resistance on the court of appeals to the legislature passing statutes that made manumission more difficult, leading the legislature to step in afterward and change the constitution in the 1850s. But the court still won in the end, as the judges continued to hold in favor of freedom.

The reason why a human being doomed to legal slavery cannot sue, is, not because he has not, in judgment or law, personal existence or capacity, but is altogether arbitrary, and springs from the felt necessity of withholding from slaves all legal rights. And therefore, the general rule is, and upon reasons of state, must be, that a slave can neither sue nor be sued. But although the law of this State considers slaves as property, yet it recognizes their personal existence, and, to a qualified extent, their natural rights. They may be emancipated by their owners; and must, of course, have a right to seek and enjoy the protection of the law in the establishment of all deeds or wills, or other legal documents of emancipation; and, so far, they must be considered as natural persons, entitled to some legal rights, whenever their owners shall have declared, in a proper manner, that they shall, either in presenti or in futuro, be free; and to this extent, the general reason of policy which disables slaves as persons, and subjects them to the condition of mere brute property, does not apply; and the reason being, the law ought also to cease.

— JUSTICE GEORGE ROBERTSON, *Catherine Bodine's Will*

CHAPTER THREE

Justice and Mercy in the Kentucky Court of Appeals

CASES OF CONTESTED WILLS that were resolved in favor of the enslaved beneficiaries could have implications years into the future.[1] Once a beneficiary became free, that freedom laid a foundation for future descendants to become part of a growing community of black working- and middle-class individuals and families. Such populations would not have existed without earlier generations of enslaved men and women becoming liberated from slavery. An example can be found in two cases discussed earlier: *Hubbard's Will* (Ky., 1831) and *Narcissa's Executors v. Wathan et al.* (Ky., 1842). Because the Kentucky Court of Appeals was willing to rule in favor of freedom and property, Narcissa's son became a free man of color prior to Emancipation.

In 1880 Austin Hubbard of Louisville, Kentucky, was a fifty-one-year-old barber living with his forty-nine-year-old wife Sarah, who "kept house." Their twenty-two-year-old daughter Sallie lived at home, as did Austin's sixty-eight-year-old mother-in-law Mary Mordica. All were described as mulattos. Their neighborhood was predominantly white working class, where the white male heads of household were carpenters, cabinet makers, pottery vendors, and blacksmiths. Hubbard's father-in-law had been an Irishman.[2] Hubbard, in turn, was named after his grandfather Austin Hubbard, a white farmer from Nelson County who left an estate to his enslaved mother Narcissa. The estate she won founded the basis of Hubbard's right to freedom years before.

On July 8, 1835, she made her last will and testament, empowering John McIsaac and Nathaniel Wickliffe to pursue the claims she had upon the elder Austin Hubbard's estate, who had hoped his estate could be used to buy her freedom from her owner, Dr. William Elliot. But as we learned in chapter 1, back in 1831 the caretaker of the estate, Thomas Wathan, colluded with Peter Sweets to defraud her, offering to pay for her freedom so that she might be manumitted, but only if she were to relinquish all claims to an estate that was "insolvent or not worth more than about as much as would pay the $350 given by them to her master for her liberation."[3] This "worthless estate" was in reality worth about $15,000.

Once Narcissa died McIsaac and Wickliffe pursued her claim for the purposes she intended: sell the estate and use the proceeds to manumit and provide for the support of Henry F. Hubbard and Austin Hubbard, the two children she bore while in slavery. Her sons were still minors owned by her former owner, Elliot. The court of appeals held for her, in an opinion written by Chief Justice George Robertson, *Narcissa's Executors v. Wathan et al.* (1842).[4] This opinion was not the first involving the manumission of Narcissa. An earlier decision written by Justice Joseph R. Underwood, *Hubbard's Will* (1831), determined the will was valid.[5] The court found that Narcissa had a greater right to the inheritance left by her father, since she was the more worthy of his two children, an illegitimate mixed-race slave daughter over an illegitimate white son. Hubbard was a "righteous father," trying to do what was right under difficult circumstances. Notwithstanding allegations that Hubbard was a drunkard, Underwood noted, "Whatever may be our feelings or detestation towards drunkenness, on account of the moral and physical evils with which it afflicts mankind, still we cannot seize upon the acts of folly, which drunkards so frequently display, and thereupon declare them incompetent to make last wills and testaments."[6]

Robertson, like Underwood, was skeptical of the argument that the men were incapacitated. He took a view similar to that taken by Underwood when challengers to a will protested the emancipation of slaves in *Reed's Will* (Ky., 1841): "the only negative facts [were] the testator's age and physical infirmities, his attachment to and emancipation of his slaves."[7] That did not mean the slaves had taken advantage of him, and in fact "the liberation of his slaves at his own death, had been his settled purpose for many years, and when there could be no question as to his capacity."[8] Because incapacitation was such a key weapon in the arsenal of challengers, one that not only denied the bequest but invalidated the will in its entirety, the court's refusal to buy the argument meant that slaves like Narcissa had a good chance at winning.

Her son Austin was born around 1819. He became free in 1848 at the age of nineteen, receiving a certificate of freedom signed by the clerk of the local courthouse. The entry into the order book described him as a bright mulatto, 5' 4½" tall, with straight brown hair that "inclined to curl," with no noticeable identifying marks.[9] He filed bond in case he should ever became a public charge. He became free because Narcissa was persistent in fighting for her financial inheritance, which provided his foundation of freedom.

The elder Austin Hubbard's case raised key questions on the right of slave manumission in the context of parental rights and responsibilities. It was one of Robertson's last judicial opinions on the subject of slave manumission in Kentucky after a judicial career spanning fourteen years, beginning in December 1829 as chief justice and ending with his April 1843 resignation.[10] In that period he wrote many of the court opinions on cases involving the manumission of slaves.[11] Robertson was well-known as an educator and treatise writer. He also served in Congress and in the state legislature. As a law professor at Transylvania University in Lexington from 1834 through

Justice George Robertson, ca. 1840. C. Frank Dunn Collection, Kentucky Historical Society.

1857 and as a treatise writer, he was a recognized leader in the legal community. For these reasons, a discussion of his ideas on slavery and the cases he wrote on the question of slave manumission is merited as an indication of how Kentucky's Court of Appeals developed as a key institution supporting manumission rights for slaves.

In the case of Narcissa's executors, Robertson highlighted slaves' vulnerability in a regime not of their making. Austin Hubbard of Bardstown died in 1823 unmarried and with no legitimate children. If Narcissa's freedom could not be bought, Hubbard's inheritance would fall to his white son, Austin F. Hubbard, also born out of wedlock. Peter Sweets was an outsider to the action who bought Narcissa's half-brother's contingent interest. It is unclear how Robertson viewed the interracialism at the heart of the case. In the earlier opinion that determined the validity of the will, Underwood had applauded Hubbard's treatment of his mixed-race slave daughter over a white illegitimate son. Nonetheless, the language of Robertson's opinion was remarkable for its solicitude and use of equity to confer an obligation to a slave. Slaves were not usually the beneficiaries of contracts capable of enforcing obligations, and they were more often property than owners of property capable of entering into contracts with others for goods and services:

> It was the equitable duty of both of them, therefore, and especially of Wathan, to disclose to Narcissa, frankly and explicitly the situation of the estate and her potential interest in it. . . . The condition of Narcissa, the tacit admissions of Wathan, and the positive proof as to Sweets, will allow no room for a rational doubt that they made a fraudulent use of their peculiar knowledge and position, and unconscientiously deceived and imposed upon an isolated victim, who had not the ordinary means of rescue or resistance.[12]

To a modern reader Robertson's views might appear liberal in protecting a vulnerable female slave, but he was operating within a tradition of liberality in manumission practices that had long existed in the state. The first Commonwealth of Kentucky constitution reflected Kentucky's history as having once been part of Virginia. Article 9 of this 1792 constitution denied the legislature the right to emancipate slaves without the permission of their owners. Legislators could not prevent immigrants from bringing their slaves with them. Perhaps in keeping with the revolutionary spirit of the time that led to flexible manumission statutes throughout the nation, the legislature was required to "pass laws to permit the owners of slaves to emancipate them, saving the rights of creditors' and preventing them from becoming chargeable to the county in which they reside."[13]

Even though settlers included Virginia aristocrats who received land grants after 1778, Kentucky eventually became more of a western state than a southern one, although its early heritage as a slave society colored its politics and law throughout the nineteenth century. Kentucky bordered the North and it developed a farming economy of small landowners; it was not a plantation economy, thus it did not benefit from slavery as much as the states of the Deep South did.[14] Thus the state legislature refused to vote secession with other southern states in 1860–61.[15] Proximity to the West and the North meant awareness of the possibilities of free white labor and manufacturing, which coincided with northern sentiments, abolitionism, support for the Whig party, and especially for Henry Clay, the prominent Whig congressman from Lexington.[16] Thus Kentucky maintained a record for being one of the Whig party's main southern strongholds.[17] These factors all might have fueled an early drive toward flexible manumission policies in the legislature.

In considering the role of judges on the Kentucky Court of Appeals, those members of the legal elite responsible for deciding just what the legislature's manumission standards were, we should attend also to the appeal of the Whigs and to the significance that the judges on the court of appeals were members of the party: "The majority of the middle and upper classes in rural areas, small towns, and large cities supported the Whigs . . . [who] portrayed themselves as the party of probity, respectability, morality, and reason—as 'the party of law, of order, of enterprise, of improvement, of beneficence, of hope, and of humanity.'"[18] Opinions written by the judges reflected this philosophy, and perspectives such as these elucidate why Justice Robertson wrote as he did.

Pursuant to the constitutional mandate to pass a manumission statute, in 1798 the state legislature made it lawful for any person by last will and testament or any other written instrument, written under seal and witnessed, or acknowledged in the local county court, "to emancipate or set free his or her slave or slaves, who shall thereupon be entirely and fully discharged from the performance of any contract entered into his servitude, and enjoy his full freedom as if they had been born free."[19] The court was authorized to demand bond for the maintenance of any freed person too aged or infirm for self-support. As for those who could support themselves, "every slave so emancipated shall have a certificate of freedom from the clerk of such court."[20]

As would be expected, all slaves were liable for the debts of an estate, and an executor could not sell a slave for any other reason; but all personal property was to be sold beforehand, since slaves were considered real estate.[21] As Thomas Morris noted, this rule was contrary to the general rule that slaves were considered personal property, which meant that when an estate was being liquidated in Kentucky's early years, slaves were to be sold as a last resort, and when manumission rights were at stake, slaves thus had the possibility of receiving greater protections under the law.[22]

Two years later the legislature did away with the requirement of a seal and recording, which simplified the manumission process, making it easier for slaves to receive their freedom."[23] This liberalization of the manumission law avoided the prerequisite of reliance upon witnesses and certification by local courts and institutions. But the manumission had to be unconditional, *Cooke v. Cooke* (Ky., 1823). Thus, a will signed by William Cooke that stated that "Peter *should* be free, on the payment of $50" (my emphasis) did not amount to an absolute manumission: "it is necessary that the writing should declare the act done, and not merely a stipulation that it shall be done conditionally, or on the happening of some contingency."[24]

Opinions written by judges on the court of appeals indicate an emphasis on paternalist protection for those deemed vulnerable and in need of care: slaves and the newly freed, in keeping with the liberal manumission standards set forth by the legislature. By a will dated November 26, 1791, when Kentucky was still part of Virginia, Edmund Lyne manumitted various slaves, three of whom were minors: Milly, James, and Lucy. Under Virginia law he could emancipate them, but the estate was liable for supporting them until they came of age. Lyne had already designated, however, that all of his cash, personal property, and real property were to be used for the support of all those he manumitted, but the question remained how much should be used to support the three children. The court in making its determination analogized their condition to free white children, "estimated from a consideration of what is generally needed for the support of other minors who are destitute of property," *Innes v. Lyne's Devisees* (Ky., 1803).[25]

This solicitude meant that the court could read the will as reflecting Lyne's rational and benevolent intentions to "mean or imply everything which [was] necessary to make their freedom a real advantage to them."[26] Thus the children should have been sent to school but not sent out to be apprenticed, because apprenticeship depended upon the goodwill of masters. Although required to give their charges "as much learning as is thought requisite to enable them advantageously to exercise their trade when they arrive at maturity . . . this requisition is too often evaded to the irreparable injury of the apprentices."[27] A classroom education would do just as well for slaves freed by will, who were more akin to apprentices required to be under care until they were old enough to support themselves.

The court exhibited similar solicitude in permitting Ruth Wilmot to bring an action against Thomas A. Thompson, with whom "she exchanged a slave named Will," for another, Harry, in 1790, *Thompson v. Wilmot* (Ky., 1809).[28] Wilmot claimed that as part of their written exchange, Thompson was to free Will within seven years; this prospect of manumission persuaded Will to leave. But Thompson reneged on his written word. Will, according to Wilmot, "instituted a suit at law . . . to recover his freedom, but had failed because the said instrument was held not to amount to an actual and formal emancipation, and the slave therefore not entitled to sue."[29] She brought action on his behalf in May 1805. The lower court found for her, and a jury awarded $691.25 in damages "to be paid by the defendant to the complainant in trust for said Negro Will."[30]

Thompson's behavior shocked the conscience of the court, indicating the extent to which early in the court's history interests of humanity were to be negotiated within the law of slavery:

> The material statements in the bill are so fully supported by evidence written and oral, that the mind cannot for a single moment withhold an assent to their absolute verity. Even the answer of Thompson does not afford a colorable pretext for withholding a performance of his engagement, solemnly made, under circumstances interesting to humanity and most obligatory upon men of good conscience and unpolluted faith. The contract in itself was not forbidden by any political institution, but is in unison with the dictates of natural right.[31]

Thompson's inexplicable and dishonorable behavior was so egregious that the court felt obligated to affirm the damages assessed by the lower court in chancery. Thus early on in the state's history the solicitude at the foundation of Kentucky's liberal manumission jurisprudence had been laid, providing a context for what was to follow: the leadership of Justice Robertson.

While Robertson was on the bench he saw the brazenness of crooks and frauds who tried wrongfully to deny slaves their freedom, and he was alert to similar injustices. He heard a case in which a chancellor had to enjoin the sale and abduction of a slave during the course of an action for freedom, *Leah et al. v. Young and Shackleford* (Ky., 1829): "To question this right would encourage fraud, oppression and violence."[32] In an 1835 law lecture he explained his philosophy about judges' obligations in deciding cases in which justice was at stake. In his view the law protected the weak and controlled the strong; it was the champion of the vulnerable.[33] Thus five years later, when he wrote an opinion in a case in which three men of color—Jonas, Turner, and Willis, once the slaves of William White—"were emancipated by the valid last will of their said former owner," he noted they were vulnerable because of their slave status, *White's Heirs v. Turner* (Ky., 1840).[34] He understood that rights to manumission could be easily extirpated by those with bad intentions, which is what happened in the White case.

One of White's sons admitted destroying the will before it could be probated, not for the purpose of denying the slaves their freedom, he said, but because the will allegedly "provided for only an ultimate liberation, depending on contingencies that had not occurred, and on prescribed conditions, which had been violated by each of the appellees."[35] Three months after White died, he and the other heirs signed a document "purporting to be a bond to the County Court . . . reciting the substance of the emancipation provision, and binding them, without proving the will, to effectuate its benevolent purposes, *as thus recited*" (original emphasis).[36]

But their apparent benevolence was phony. The testator's sons did not have any sound basis in law to destroy the will: White had not been declared unsound, and his will had not been declared invalid. But, significantly, the witnesses to the will testified "that the one they attested contained provisions essentially different from the pretended recital in the ostensible bond, and such as entitled the appellees to be free in September 1834."[37] Robertson blasted the connivers: "All the persons thus concurring in the suppression of the will, were thereby instrumental in illegally prolonging the servitude of the appellees. And as they must be presumed to have thus acted, for their own unjust profit, and with a full knowledge of the legal right of the appellees, they all subjected themselves to liability for damages."[38] Jonas, Turner, and Willis sought $500 each in damages, the estimated value of their services; Robertson ruled they were entitled to it.

Even if the conditions for manumission had been met, it is likely that Robertson would still have favored immediate manumission over manumission to take place in the future. In another case, *Dunlap and Collins v. Archer* (Ky., 1838), Robertson was willing to view a document purporting prospective manumission "upon good behavior" over a period of seven years' service as valid for emancipating a slave, rejecting the dissent's opinion that to follow the letter of the law, there should have been a separately executed document upon the expiration of the term. Justice Ephraim M. Ewing explained, "I certainly entertain great doubts, and incline to the opinion, strongly, that the instrument as proven was an executory contract, binding Lane to give a writing of emancipation, at the expiration of the time, in case of faithful service; and cannot be construed an executed writing, of emancipation, within the provisions of our statute."[39] Thus in the view of the majority it was plausible that the document alone could manumit under the law.

Robertson clearly supported the rights of owners to free their slaves and leave them bequests of property, and he clearly saw himself as having a unique role when hearing cases where manumission was at stake, as he stated in a public address: "Virtuous and enlightened jurists are the peculiar guardians of the commonwealth, because law is the panoply of all that is most cherished and endearing among men. Without good laws, honestly administered, there could be no security for life, liberty, reputation or property."[40] But the unscrupulous found it very easy to interfere and deny what had been the owners' wishes. In writing decisions benefitting former slaves, Robertson was helped, as was discussed earlier, by Kentucky having a flexible manumission policy that offered room for judges to maneuver.

As for Underwood, the judge who wrote the opinion upholding Narcissa's inheritance rights and who appeared to be liberal on manumission, insofar as he manumitted all his slaves and upheld the rights of the mixed-race Narcissa as inheritor over her white half-brother, he had a similar reaction to mixed-race relationships. In one case heirs at law sued to overturn on the basis of insanity, a will that liberated several of Philip Patton's slaves. The lower court didn't overturn and the court of appeals affirmed, *Patton's Heirs v. Patton's Executors* (Ky., 1831): "The fact that the deceased evinced an inclination to marry the slave, Grace, whom he liberated, is not a stronger evidence of insanity than the practice of rearing children by a slave without marriage; a practice but too common, as we all know, from the numbers of our mulatto population. However degrading, such things are; and however repugnant to the institutions of society, and the moral law, they prove more against the taste than the intellect."[41]

Thus Robertson and Underwood were caught between solicitude for owners' prerogatives and dismay over unconventional exercises of those prerogatives, in the form of interracial liaisons. Yet Robertson's continued solicitude for the well-being of those hoping for freedom, even where no biological ties between owner and slave could be found, can be explained as his recognition of paternalistic sentiments. Righteous slave owners, not only the righteous fathers of the enslaved, should have the right to manumit when they saw fit.

But perhaps this solicitude was not unusual for judges in the state. Robertson's colleague Justice Samuel S. Nicholas held in an early case, *Young v. Slaughter* (Ky., 1834), that it was obligatory for the executor and son of the late Colonel Gabriel Slaughter, John H. Slaughter, to provide a former slave, John Young, with "food and raiment during his life."[42] Young sued when he did not receive the support he believed he was entitled to. Slaughter's argument for withholding support was that "Young [was] able-bodied and competent, with proper industry, to feed and clothe himself"; he felt Young was only to be taken care of once "he became too old or infirm to procure them by his own industry."[43] Even though the evidence showed that Young was old, he could still support himself; fifty dollars a year was all that would be required for his upkeep. Thus the lower court dismissed the bill, siding with Slaughter.

Nicholas, in writing for a reversal, explained: "We cannot concur in this construction. It looks to us more like amending the will, than construing it. The language is simply, that he shall be furnished with food and raiment during his life. There is nothing in any part of the will, qualifying the import of this language."[44] But that did not mean that "Young should be clothed and fed like a gentleman, . . . only like a negro; but we can find nothing in the testator's language, to warrant the idea that he was not to be clothed and fed at all."[45] In a world in which there was no social safety net for a former slave like Young, the will provided a modicum of support.

In this case the appeals court's sense of paternalism held sway. But it was a worldview that presumed slaves childlike, even incompetent. Nicholas imagined that the late Colonel Slaughter might have been concerned that Young would not be able to support himself, as a result of "indolence or dissipation . . . in which event his emancipation might prove a curse, instead of the boon it was intended to be."[46] This was a motive the court applauded: "We can understand not only the motive, but also duly appreciate those feelings of a kind owner, which would prompt the endeavor to secure his slave . . . the indispensable necessities of life."[47]

Considering Robertson's paternalism and his tendency to support emancipation, he was thus unwilling in an action for freedom to let stand presumptions that would deny petitioners the right to assert their claims. The petitioner, Polly McMinnis, was the daughter of an enslaved woman, born after Pennsylvania's gradual emancipation statute. The Kentucky court needed to determine whether she was free as a result of the statute, and whether her Kentucky owner improperly denied her right to freedom? Robertson affirmed the trial court's refusal to instruct the jury that the petitioner's thirty years in bondage should make a presumption of her slave status, *Gentry v. McMinnis* (Ky., 1835). The statute of limitations did not apply in this action for freedom, and her color was not presumptive, that is, her appearance did not immediately identify her as a black woman: her opponent, Gentry, was unable to assert that her color made her a slave. It was up to the members of the jury to listen and decide for themselves.[48]

This rejecting of presumptions that would deny freedom could apply to those who would deny former slaves monetary bequests to which they were entitled. Early in Robertson's career, the court heard a case in which a slave owner, Thomas Hart, liberated his slave, Joe, by will, and devised him $200, "to assist him in buying his wife."[49] Seventeen years later Joe filed a bill in the chancery court against the estate's representatives to enforce payment of the bequest. One of the representatives, Hart, was unwilling to sell her, and thus the purpose of the devise was ineffective and void. Beyond that, they argued, Joe lived on property owned by the widow, receiving small sums of money on occasion. Because this amounted to the sum of the bequest, it was a setoff. The lower court dismissed Joe's bill, on the basis of lapse of time and a presumption of payment.

Robertson disagreed, *Joe v. Hart's Executors* (Ky., 1829). Mrs. Thomas Hart never charged Joe for living on her property and considered the money she gave him as a gift not to be repaid: "As he lived with her, and was generally devoted to her service, it would be expected that she would, at least, furnish him occasionally with trifling sums, to enable him to buy small comforts. This was right and natural."[50] Neither the statute of limitations nor laches applied. Moreover, Robertson found irrelevant the fact that the owner of Joe's wife did not have any interest in selling her. Perhaps he might sell in the future: "Joe is entitled to the $200 before he shall have purchased his wife, because it was devised to him" in aiding him to make the purchase.[51]

But Robertson's ruling in this case did not mean that all newly freed slaves always inherited the sums of money they thought they were entitled to receive. The legislature passed a special act declaring that Zachariah Conclude should become free and inherit the estate of his father, Isaac Conclude, a free man of color who died without legal heirs free and capable of taking his property. This in the eyes of the court "entitled him to the civil rights guaranteed to the white man."[52] Zachariah filed suit in chancery that the estate was worth $2,500, funds that were in the hands of the administrator, Williamson. It is unclear where he got that figure, but Robertson read the evidence at trial as supporting the administrator's claim instead, that the estate was worth $440.75, of which $400 had been expended on the purchase and freedom of Isaac's daughter (Zachariah's sister). The estate could not provide Zachariah any money because of the estate's debts and because Williamson had not been paid for performing his duties of administration.[53]

Reading Zachariah as being greedy, Robertson proclaimed, "and he is now endeavoring to abuse the liberty thus acquired, by denying the defendant's right to apply a portion of the derelict funds of her father to the liberation of this same Zachariah's sister. . . . The administrator might have sold him before the date of the act if he had been influenced by cupidity."[54] One might wonder whether the estate ever had $2,500 in assets; that how Zachariah arrived at that figure was unknown is indicative of the disabilities Zachariah experienced in trying to assert his claim. He was not free at the time of his father's death and was thus barred from inheriting without an act of the legislature. Thus he was incapable of taking immediate control over his father's affairs.

This was ultimately the disability experienced by all who would claim bequests of freedom and property. Even though judges could be solicitous of their demands for freedom, the soon-to-be freed were still vulnerable to the executors, caretakers, and challengers opposing their interests. Thus, the estate of Enoch Smith became entered in litigation over a benevolent purchase and sale of freedom. Before he died Enoch Smith liberated all his slaves. Yet a few years later he bought Sarah, the enslaved wife of Ben, a free man of color, reselling her to her husband in 1809, taking promissory notes for payment of the debt. A deed of emancipation for her and her children Milton and Fanny was prepared thereafter in 1813. Its sufficiency was verified by a lawyer engaged by Smith, and the deed was acknowledged by Ben in the county court.[55] Problems arose when Smith died in 1825 and the executors found that Ben failed to pay the purchase price before dying intestate in 1818. They seized Sarah and her children, hoping to sell them for the payment of the debt.

Ferguson, as an executor of the estate, surprisingly had no right to seize any of them, in the eyes of Robertson, *Ferguson et al. v. Sarah et al.* (Ky., 1830). The executors were not personal creditors that the estate might have owed money, and Smith had waived any right he might have had to any payment owed: "E. Smith lived several years after the emancipation, during which time, he recognized Sarah, Milton and Fanny, as free persons. In his will, he did not mention them, or any one of them."[56] He did not mention the debt as being owed him. The deed of emancipation was effective.

A slave could also assert a right to wages for his service prior to the adjudication of a will's validity, according to *Black v. Meaux* (Ky.,

1836). This was in reversal of the lower-court judge "having virtually instructed the jury to find for the defendant" because, according to Robertson:

> Humphrey Black, one of the persons who had been thus emancipated, having lived with John Woodson Meaux, and worked for him from the time of the testator's death to that of the decision upon the will by this Court—sued him . . . for compensation for his services; and having, on the trial . . . proved that the defendant, had on different occasions, . . . said, though not to him, that he would pay him for his labor in the event of the establishment of the will by the judgment of this Court.[57]

Ordering a remand, Robertson wrote that the jury should have heard the evidence presented by Black: "If the plaintiff was a free man from the testator's death, whatever may be the true rule of law as to the legal right to compensation . . . we cannot doubt that, as there was, at least, a moral obligation to pay for the services which appear to have been valuable, and should not have been presumed to be gratuitous."[58]

The right to freedom was of much greater importance than a former slave's history of working in bondage, and the chancery courts were charged to look out for the dispossessed, according to the opinion in *Aleck v. Tevis* (Ky., 1836):

> [D]o not analogy and fitness furnish sufficient ground for maintaining a bill in chancery for establishing and securing the freedom of a rational being, disfranchised and subjugated by a fellow-being, to whom public opinion, the organization of society, or other accident has given the power to govern him as a slave, and disable him from understanding or using the ordinary means of manifesting and maintaining his rights?[59]

This meant that those who might gain their freedom pursuant to a will deserved greater protections. They were primary beneficiaries above all others, empowered to defend their rights in court. This was significant because nothing in the 1798 Kentucky statute indicated how the newly freed were to be treated when the estate might not have sufficient funds to cover the decedent's debts. Thus the judges had room to maneuver and could base their decisions on their own sense of justice. Justice Ewing admitted that slaves could be sacrificed to satisfy the demands of creditors, even though freedom might be at stake. He nonetheless could hold contrary to that view, *Nancy (a colored woman) v. Snell* (Ky., 1838): "[Slaves], when emancipated by will . . . occupy the double character of property and legatees, or quasi legatees."[60] He noted further, "and as freedom is a legacy, above all price, humanity, justice and the spirit of our laws, inculcate the propriety of placing them in the most favored class of legatees."[61]

According to the court then, a sale of slaves did not stand in a case in which a slave, Nancy, had been freed with her children, Charles and Richard Hamilton, in Maryland by the last will and testament of Ann Burgess, but all were then sold by the executors to Osborn, a Kentucky resident, who then sold them to Snell. If there were any debts to be paid off the estate should have been made to pay prior to any sale of the slaves entitled to freedom, and if any were to be sold it should have been only for a term of years to pay off the debt. But in Nancy's situation her prior claim was important enough that the buyers should have exercised caveat emptor. As Justice Ewing explained, Osborn was remiss in his duty in not determining Nancy's status as a woman entitled to freedom. He could have accessed the public records and discovered all the pertinent facts of her status. As Marshall later noted in *Snead v. David* (Ky., 1840), if a slave has a right to freedom the slave "can only be subjected to the debts of the testator by means of a direct proceeding . . . against him; in which the necessity or propriety, and manner, of subjecting him to the satisfaction of the debt, and the extent to which he should be subjected, may be ascertained."[62]

This right to freedom was to be protected at all costs, even though a will bore a date subsequent to the decedent's death; mere typographical errors could not defeat a valid will, *Susan (a colored woman) v. Ladd* (Ky., 1837). It was particularly important to protect those rights if there was a hint of fraud, as the court found in *Boyce v. Nancy* (Ky., 1836). Robertson perceived shady dealings in the actions of an administrator colluding to defraud the estate of a recently deceased woman, Rebecca Ring. He carefully scrutinized all the evidence submitted and found that the creditor making claims had already been paid. If there were still debts outstanding there was money to pay it without selling Nancy, a slave once owned by Ring. Moreover, said Robertson, "in fact, as well as in law, the bond given to Troth, after all those settlements, was the personal debt of [the executor,] and he had no semblance of authority to sell the appellee."[63] Nancy was supposed to have been freed at age twenty-one but was kept in bondage instead for more than twenty years. Robertson suggested that the executor hoped to keep her in bondage in Kentucky by taking her out of Maryland, where she had been born and owned by Ring, and where the will established her right to freedom.

Robertson's solicitude did not extend, however, to cases in which the intent to manumit was not clearly stated, *Jameson v. Emaline* (Ky., 1837). Although there was a bill of sale that purported to free Maria after fifteen years and to liberate on their reaching the age of thirty any children she might have had in the interim, because there was no provision in the will for any of Maria's grandchildren, Robertson denied the manumission of Emaline, a child of Maria's daughter Nancy. He stated "as no provision was made respecting the grand children born while their mothers were slaves, we have no authority to supply the omission by speculating on the probable cause of it, or by presuming that the parties intended what they have not even intimated, and which . . . is altogether inconsistent with the legal effect of what they expressly declared."[64] If there had been a clear intent to liberate any of Maria's grandchildren, Emaline would have won her freedom.

We might ask whether Robertson or any of the other judges would have seen their opinions that were ostensibly solicitous of slaves as an indication of anything more than deciding cases solely upon the rule of law, regardless of any sentiments they had about slavery and slaves. In an introductory lecture on law Robertson once explained that law students should think about questions of "universal jurisprudence," described as "the knowledge of things human and divine, the science of what is just and unjust."[65] Yet as was mentioned earlier, Robertson's opinions in many instances certainly read today as if he had some sentimentality where the rights of slaves were concerned. Arguably his own views on slavery are important for developing an understanding.

In various public speeches Robertson did not speak about his history as a slave owner or how he treated his own slaves, and it is unclear whether he ever manumitted any of his, but in an 1834 Fourth of July address he indicated his perspective on slavery in the United States:

The philanthropist has still also to lament, that a curse imposed on our ancestors when in colonial subjection, still lingers among us. Domestic slavery cannot be suddenly abolished in all the States, consistent with the welfare of either the black man or the white. A premature effort of inconsiderate humanity might be disastrous, and would certainly tend to defeat or retard the ultimate object of every good and wise man—universal emancipation. But we feel that public sentiment, public policy, and individual interest, are all conspiring to extirpate the great household evil, and will, in convenient time, and in some just and eligible mode, satisfactory to all, banish it forever from our land.[66]

Fearful of the rabidity among both abolitionists and proslavery advocates, Robertson sought the middle ground between immediate emancipation of all slaves and gradualism, a position described by the historian Harold D. Tallant as one common among conservative reformers.[67] As Robertson wrote, "he would rejoice to see all men, of every color and clime, equal in privileges and endowments, and well qualified for the peaceful enjoyment of civil, social and religious liberty and light."[68] But slavery existed, nonetheless, not through the actions of man but through the natural order that God ordained: "a wise and inscrutable Providence had otherwise ordained, and no act or policy of man can change the purpose of God."[69] He saw slavery as a benevolent regime in which everyone benefited: the white race's interest in security and the black's interest in happiness and safety.[70] As a civilizing factor its effects were extraordinary: "And who can venture to presume that negro slavery in America may have not been sanctioned by Heaven as the most fitting means for effecting the providential end of saving and ennobling the doomed African race?"[71]

Perhaps owners who sought to manumit believed the enslaved men and women were civilized enough to exercise the rights of free people. That might have been the reason Robertson was more willing to hold for the rights of former slaves. Because owners understood the characters and ability of the enslaved men and women they owned, others should defer to their wishes to manumit: "one person's right is that which all other persons are ordered or commanded by law to let him have and enjoy."[72] Perhaps manumission on a case-by-case basis was the best means of effectuating the eventual abolition of the entire regime:

> He had never considered slavery in itself a blessing. He had always felt it as a curse to the white race. But as it exists in Kentucky, it is not now within the compass of human wisdom, philanthropy and power all combined, to adopt any system of compulsive liberation which will be practicable, just, safe, and sure.[73]

Perhaps, then, Robertson viewed his opinions on manumission as contributing to universal emancipation. As individual slaveholders took advantage of Kentucky's flexible manumission laws, liberating their slaves during life or at death, and as courts upheld the wills, slavery would no longer exist, or the numbers of slaves in the jurisdiction could be decreased to such an extent that abolition might be a feasible policy. He believed the legislature should not abolish slavery outright because the numbers of slaves and slaveholders in the state were substantial enough that such a policy would be controversial. Instead, the legislature and the judiciary should support not only emancipation policies that would coincide with a goal of gradual abolition but those that would ban the importation of slaves into the state. The nonimportation bill passed in 1833, because many thought, as did Robertson, that Kentucky had too many slaves. Only immigrants and those inheriting slaves from elsewhere could bring out-of-state slaves into the jurisdiction; thus the slave population would inevitably decrease.[74] Nonetheless, the 1849 constitution dropped the nonimportation law, the result of proslavery interests in the convention: "a majority of the delegates were slaveowners."[75]

After Robertson resigned from the bench in 1843 the court continued the trend of supporting flexible manumission polices, ruling on the side of freedom and humanity. That continuing trend meant, however, that the population of free blacks increased in Kentucky in the years leading up to the war, resulting in a belated effort to end all manumission of slaves in the state by the 1850s. This meant that on the eve of the Civil War Kentucky was aligning itself with other slave jurisdictions in the Deep South that had limited slave manumissions decades before.[76]

Building on earlier precedents that refused to limit a slave's claim to freedom on the basis of laches (the doctrine that stale claims could not be litigated), the court found instead that laches applied to claimants who sat on their rights in the face of slaves' interests in manumission, *Wood's Executors v. Wickliffe* (Ky., 1844). Nathaniel Wickliffe sued Nathan B. Wood in 1824. After Wood died in 1834, his will was recorded. Wickliffe pursued a court order reviving the suit the following year in 1835, and only served it upon the executors in 1837. Wickliffe gained a judgment of $3,000 in 1841 and then filed a claim against the estate for the sale of five of Wood's slaves and others who had been freed by the will: Ann, Eliza, Elizabeth, Bertrand, and Louisa. It was inexplicable why the case sat on the docket for more than ten years, only to be revived a few years after Wood's death, with no notice to the executors that any claim had ever existed prior to the filing of Wickliffe's request to revive. The filing of the suit alone was not notice of the claim, and the slaves freed almost ten years before could not now simply be reenslaved and sold. Instead, serious due process issues had to be surmounted before they could be sold:

> The liberated slaves were devisees, and directly and vitally interested in this controversy. They were necessary parties, and should have been brought regularly before the Court, and as several of them were infants, a guardian should have been appointed for them, who was competent, and would undertake to defend for them; no answer was filed, and so far as appears from the record, no defense of any kind was made for any of them. We cannot admit that the mere levying of an attachment upon infant devisees of the character of these individuals, is bringing them before the Court, so as to authorize a decree against them.[77]

In the same period in Kentucky, slaves seeking to assert their rights to freedom ran the risk that others might try to thwart their actions in the courts by removing them from the jurisdiction while their cases were pending, leading to the legislature passing a penal statute that made such conduct a misdemeanor punishable by fines between $500 and $2,000. In an indictment brought before the Jefferson Circuit Court pursuant to this statute, failing to allege criminal intent proved fatal, *Commonwealth v. Stout* (Ky., 1847). The indictment claimed "defendants attempted to remove from the Commonwealth of Kentucky, Nancy, a person of color, having a suit pending for freedom in the Louisville Chancery Court."[78] That intent was not alleged meant that the defendants were not blameworthy because "persons of color, under our laws, are held in slavery; they are the subjects of sale and transfer, and individuals may purchase and remove them, even during the pendency of a suit for their freedom, without any knowledge that in so doing, they are acting illegally."[79] To prosecute there had to be proof of a guilty mind, willful knowledge, and intent to break the law, but the prosecution did not make any allegations of proof.

But mens rea was clear in cases of destroyed wills as a precursor for wrongful behavior, *Mullins v. Wall* (Ky., 1848). B. Mullins, who was both a subscribing witness to a will and an heir of his late sister, Rebecca Mullins, perjured himself in presenting her will for probate by saying that he did not witness and sign it in her presence. (It was shown that he had in fact witnessed and signed the will in her presence, only to destroy it once his testimony resulted in the will being rejected for probate.) Mullins then claimed rights to the slaves Cain and Dorcas, colluding with a brother to defraud them of their right to freedom. Taking advantage of the death of the slaves' mother, who had successfully sued for her freedom, the men seized them as slaves, when they had been living with their mother as free people of color. The Mullins men proposed to "purchase them and run them off to a distant State, where they could not establish their freedom."[80] But the court found they were freed by the will.

The Kentucky court was willing to read the statutory requirements for emancipation by will broadly in *Orchard v. David (a free man of color)* (Ky., 1846), so that a clause in a will that did not emancipate forthright, but which predicated manumission solely upon $400 payment, was sufficient to emancipate David, Jinny, and their daughter

Mary Jane, the slaves of Alexander Orchard. The newly freed slaves were to give security for the debt, and the money was to come from the children of the testator. Yet it appears they were to receive other funds: "surely he possessed the power, by a codicil . . . to take the excess over four hundred dollars, from his children, and give it to the slaves."[81] The court took this view even though the statute required manumission be clearly fulfilled through the deeds purporting to liberate, and even though in general slaves had no right to own property, much less $400 in cash.

The court reasoned that their slave status was a mere temporary disability, not an absolute bar against inheritance rights. Thus, the estate belonging to a free man of color, Jacob Cox, could be inherited by his daughters who were in slavery at the time his will was made, *Darcus v. Crump* (Ky., 1846). He gave his wife Mary one third of his estate. The other two thirds of his estate was to be used in purchasing his two daughters Darcus and Charlotte. Upon Mary's death the two would inherit the remainder. Mary died before he did, and his daughters were living in Virginia and Tennessee at the time of his death. Daniel Crump, one of the executors, sold the estate: 150 acres of land and personal property. He purchased and emancipated both women and bought the land himself. Darcus and Charlotte challenged the sale as fraudulent.

Daniel Crump argued in turn that because all the beneficiaries—Mary, Darcus and Charlotte—were slaves at Jacob's death, they could not inherit, and the bequests failed for an inability to vest. The court did not subscribe to that argument: "But we are by no means prepared to sustain the position, that because the estate did not and could not vest while the complainants were slaves, it would not vest upon their manumission."[82] Jacob Cox had left a considerable estate to his family, and his daughters were eligible to take their share upon their emancipation. Not only did the court find the sale of the land fraudulent but it ruled that the administrative fees Crump claimed were "improper and exhorbitant."[83] The court held the land should be given to the women.

By the 1850s the state legislature began tightening manumission laws in an effort to decrease the size of the free black population. At the same time it took contrary positions. It also codified various holdings developed by the high court over the rights of creditors when the emancipation interests of slaves were at stake. The legislature did this to protect creditors by postponing emancipation and ensuring that estates' debts would be paid. But they also put in place greater protections for the rights of slaves to be freed by will to ensure that their right to freedom would not be unduly sacrificed and lost.

Thus the General Assembly of Kentucky required that in cases in which slaves would be emancipated by last will and testament, all slaves to be emancipated would be considered assets for the executors to use in paying the debts. No slave could be emancipated and given a certificate of freedom without the assent of the representatives that the estate's assets were sufficient for paying the debts. If an emancipation interest was at stake and the assets were insufficient, slaves could be sold only upon a bill filed in the court of chancery, with the slaves as necessary parties. A sale of the slaves could be pursued only as a last resort if a hire for a term of years was insufficient.[84]

Executors were under obligation to emancipate as soon as it was clear that estates had sufficient funds for paying debts. But until such time as that was ascertained from a testator's records, an executor could hire out slaves. If the estate of the testator was sufficient to pay the debts, the funds of the hire belonged to the slaves. If the slaves thought emancipation was wrongfully withheld, they could file a bill in chancery to force the executor to act. If the validity of the will at stake was being challenged, the chancellor was required to prevent the slaves from leaving the state and was to hire them out pending the resolution of the matter. Those challenging the will were to file bond to indemnify those defending the will's validity. If the will was found valid and the slaves' labor unnecessary to pay the estate's debts, they were entitled to the money from the hire, and before any slave was to be freed, the county courts were to demand bond and security that the slave would not become a public charge.[85]

The changes in the law presented challenges to those seeking manumission. In the April 1850 term of the Madison County Court, five slaves freed by the will of Humphrey Tunstall probated in February of that year offered their bonds with security as required by law. One of the executors refused to manumit, and the court rejected the slaves' offer of bond: the court did not "permit the bond to be executed and to grant certificates of freedom."[86] The slaves then filed a bill in the court of equity against the executors, to which the executors replied:

> [T]hey neither assented or dissented . . . but that they withheld their assent on account of the short period which had elapsed from the testator's death, and not being fully acquainted with his affairs, they were unwilling to incur responsibility by immediate and absolute assent, and because they had in fact taken no control over the complainants, but had let them go about as free persons.[87]

The high court agreed that the county court should have allowed them to execute their bonds: "their rights could not be prejudiced by the improper refusal of their offer . . . in equity the offer made in good faith vested the right of freedom."[88] The slaves had offered to execute their bonds within a reasonable time, and court ruled that the executors should have assented: "They admit that the other estate of the testator, beside the seven negroes conditionally emancipated, was, and is, amply sufficient to pay his debts."[89]

It is unclear whether the executors acted in bad faith in refusing the slaves' bond, but the contingent remainderman, Humphrey T. Hill, the person who would have inherited if the bequests failed, might have. He had no right to charge the executors for the slaves' hire for the time when they were permitted to go free: "the statute of 1841 . . . expressly enacts what would otherwise be the dictate of equity, that the hire shall be for the benefit of the emancipated slave."[90] Hill was the only person opposing the slaves' emancipation, and since his opposition failed to be sustained by the court "it was certainly right to decree against him all the cost of the complainants in their contest with him."[91]

But although slaves could bring an action for freedom, that right did not extend to enforcing a contract for emancipation, *Major v. Winn's Adm'r* (Ky., 1852). The slave named Major claimed "that Martin, his former owner, when he sold him to [Winn], the defendant's intestate, did not intend to sell him as a slave for the rest of his life, but only during the life of the purchaser, at whose death he was to be free."[92] The court found significant the fact that there was no writing in the bill of sale to indicate "the verbal contract between the parties."[93] Yet Major had no legal capacity to have a contract for his emancipation enforced by the court. The law in effect only limited his right to sue for manumission under a specific writing, for example, a will that clearly set forth his emancipation.

That did not mean, however, that a clause in a will that was advisory but not mandatory could emancipate, *Hawkins v. Hawkins* (Ky., 1852): "It is my will and desire that my wife Lucy should have my negroes during her life or widowhood, with full power to emancipate them all before or at her death, as they, said negroes, arrive at the age of thirty-one years. It is my wish and desire that my wife Lucy should emancipate said negroes as above directed."[94] In this case the court ruled that the widow was under no obligation to emancipate if she did not want to, since her late husband had said only he hoped she would do as he requested, rather than require her to do so. The slaves hoping to become emancipated thus had no cause of action.

Moreover, an oral agreement to emancipate between John M. Patton and his slave Norris could not be enforced, *Norris (of color) v. Patton's Adm'r* (Ky., 1855), and a bequest of $200 each given to the slaves Dodson and Spicy by their late owner Humphrey Jones did not imply grants of freedom and rights to inherit the funds.[95] They could only inherit if the will explicitly emancipated them, *Jones v. Lipscomb* (Ky., 1853).[96] Just because a slave was permitted to act as though she were free did not grant freedom if there was no paper that purported to manumit, *Anderson et al. v. Crawford* (Ky., 1854).[97] The plaintiffs claimed their rights to freedom on the basis that their mother Milly had been permitted to live as a free person for twenty years. Milly was the enslaved daughter of B. Ray, who devised her to Mrs. Crawford, his legitimate white daughter and Milly's half-sister.

By 1857, however, mere deed could not emancipate in the Commonwealth of Kentucky. When Ormsby Gray executed and delivered a deed of emancipation to his slave Adam he made a mistake, *Smith v. Adam* (Ky., 1857). Under older rules that alone would have sufficed, but the 1850 constitution changed the landscape of manumission by making certain requirements of the assembly: "They shall pass laws to permit owners of slaves to emancipate them, saving the rights of creditors, and to prevent them from remaining in this State after they are emancipated."[98] As a result, the court noted in *Smith* that owners had stricter threshold requirements: all deeds had to be "acknowledged or proved by two subscribing witnesses in the county court."[99] The old rules of informal manumission that existed since Kentucky's early history were rejected in favor of official policies that required state sanction beyond the certification requirement of 1842 that the freed person would not become a public charge.[100]

Granted, the rules passed by the state legislature pursuant to the constitution were not as strict as those in other jurisdictions. As justification for the new rules, the court pointed to "the rapid increase of that class of population within the State, and the evils to be apprehended therefrom."[101] Thus, the 1850 constitution explained: "The General Assembly shall pass laws providing that any free negro or mulatto hereafter immigrating to, any slave hereafter emancipated in, and refusing to leave this State, or having left, shall return and settle within this State, shall be deemed guilty of a felony, and punished by confinement in the Penitentiary thereof."[102]

Thus, fears of an increasing free black population threatening the white populace resulted in concrete measures to limit that increase. Although the census data indicate the population of free blacks was increasing, it is unclear just how real the threat was. In 1830 there were 517,787 whites; slaves numbered 165,213, and there were only 4,917 free blacks. Ten years later there were 590,253 whites, 7,317 free blacks, and 182,258 slaves. By 1860 there were 919,484 whites, 10,684 free blacks, and 225,483 slaves.[103] With the number of whites in the community increasing at a higher rate, the number of free blacks was still such a small proportion of the overall community as to be insignificant. Moreover, the constitution did not bar immigrants from bringing their slaves into the state "so long as [they] shall be continued in slavery by the laws of this state."[104] Official state policy thus guaranteed an increasing black population of slaves, even though those newly emancipated were required to leave.

Forced emigration was particularly dangerous for free blacks with enslaved spouses. Free persons of color could own their enslaved spouses, parents, or descendants. Under the new rules passed by the legislature subsequent to the 1850 constitution, however, Stephen Kyler could not emancipate his wife Cynthia; she would have to leave the state. His former owner, Joseph Kyler, was advised by a lawyer who told him he should sell her to Stephen so they could remain in Kentucky. But remaining in Kentucky meant they could be separated, because the wife of a free negro could be sold for the execution of her husband's debts, *Kyler and Wife v. Dunlap* (Ky., 1857).

Luck was with those who were manumitted prior to the assembly passing legislation pursuant to the new constitution's requirements. Those so manumitted escaped deportation, solely on technicalities regarding prohibitions against ex post facto laws, because what had been perfectly appropriate in an earlier time threatened to become illegal with the new laws in effect. The ex post facto possibilities were especially important because the terms of a deed of emancipation could be prospective: meant to take effect at a later date. Delphia Jackson was emancipated by a deed signed by her mother and dated October 26, 1850, four months after the 1850 constitution set forth that the assembly should limit the right of the newly manumitted to remain in Kentucky. That matter of timing was the crux of the case. Because no legislation had been passed yet, the 1798 law was in effect and a looser standard was used that permitted manumission and the right to remain. Delphia inherited her mother's house and property, *Jackson v. Collins* (Ky., 1855).[105]

Kitty, on the other hand, was not required to leave the state even though her emancipation took effect five years after the 1850 constitution. She had been sold by William T. Winston to Joseph Chambers in 1843 to become free in August 1855. Once the term expired she lived freely until 1857, when the local county court in Boone "placed her in the custody of a trustee to be hired out" so that enough funds could be "raised to defray the expense of her removal to some place out of this State."[106] Resisting the order, Kitty appealed the trial court's decision to place her in custody. The court of appeals agreed with her, *Kitty v. Commonwealth* (Ky., 1857):

> Her right to freedom was created and vested by the execution and
> delivery of the bill of sale from Winston to Chambers, and existed

prior to the adoption either of the present constitution or Revised Statutes. The postponement of the enjoyment of such right neither impaired the right itself nor affected its enjoyment in such manner as the laws then subsisting allowed.[107]

Executors who argued that manumission was impossible under the new rules could object only if the estate couldn't pay its debts and the slaves to be manumitted were thus affected, or "because of the insufficiency of the surety in the bond which was required by the court," *Davis v. Reeves* (Ky., 1859).[108] If the bond provided by Maria Reeves, a newly freed person, was insufficient that she would not become a ward of any local county or of the decedent's estate, the executor could object, but not because he imagined he could not manumit under the new rules. Using the 1850 constitution as an excuse, the executor complained the laws were confusing and that he hadn't manumitted Reeves "because he believed the emancipation and the issual of the certificate had to be controlled, not by the laws in force when the will was recorded, but by the Revised Statutes."[109]

But under the circumstances the executor's objection was groundless. Maria Reeves was emancipated by Amos Davis's will recorded in 1835, with her emancipation to take place upon her reaching the age of thirty. She provided bond with adequate security to the Montgomery County Court in January 1858, but no provision was made for her removal from Kentucky, even though the new law required her deportation. Nonetheless, the court ruled that the new law did not affect her, reasoning that the estate's assets were sufficient to pay off the debts, and the new rules were not even in effect when the will was recorded. Thus the executor was deemed to have acted incorrectly in refusing the assent required by law before manumission could occur.

By the 1850s, then, Kentucky had only put into place the restrictions on manumission that other southern states had in place for at least a generation, such as requiring deportation or requiring witnesses to manumissions where there was no such policy before. But even under those circumstances manumission under the new system was still possible. The legislature did not undertake to be the sole arbiter of petitions to manumit, thus enabling owners to exercise their own prerogatives. The changes in the state's law, taking place on the eve of the Civil War, are significant in light of Kentucky's history as a border state. Perhaps because Kentucky remained neutral throughout the war, moderation was exercised by the judicial system, with legislators and judges like Robertson trying to find a middle ground.

As a result, the language as found in the judges' opinions and their rulings on manumission indicate the nuances of law and language. After the legislature—the body of government most responsible for setting forth the statutory law on slavery—passed the first manumission statute in 1798, it took more than fifty years for it to institute draconian measures that curtailed manumission. It passed its strictest measure only upon constitutional mandate that forced the legislature to act. Even then, the judges on the court were unwilling to cooperate fully with the tightening binds of proslavery restrictions. They used their consciences, their sense of right and wrong, to blunt the edges of legislation and counteract the will of proslavery southerners who opposed manumission in the Commonwealth of Kentucky. They did this on a case-by-case basis.

Justice O'Neall of South Carolina, introduced in chapter 1, indicated a similar willingness to consider manumission case by case, notwithstanding popular pressure to reinforce the demands of the formal law of slavery: denial of freedom, reinforcement of white supremacy, and protection of white wealth. He is discussed further in chapter 5, in the context of the case of Elijah Willis. Chapter 4 considers a case from a different jurisdiction, *Mitchell v. Wells* in Mississippi, as an example of countervailing influence. That chapter considers judges who were less willing to reject the demands of the formal law of slavery, particularly when the legislature exerted such influence on manumission from the beginning of the state's history. The judges responded differently to rising abolitionist fervor: they followed the legislature's lead and intervened to protect the white community, even when the legislature did not clearly state a change in policy.

Changing policies explain another significant point in the context of manumission and the use of wills. These fueled the push toward using geography to achieve the desired result through the legal system. Thus geography was important not only as a matter of different states' policies—for example, states that bordered the North as opposed to the states of the Deep South, where reliance upon slaves for the cultivation of cotton was greatest and where there were greater numbers of slaves—but for the purposes of planning manumission in the context of the will. Feeling pressured, testators like Elijah Willis and Edward Wells sent their favored slaves out of the state.

The State of Ohio, forgetful of her constitutional obligations to the whole race . . . chooses to take into her embrace, as citizens, the neglected race, who by common consent of the States united, were regarded, at the formation of our government, as an inferior caste, incapable of the blessings of free government.

—JUDGE WILLIAM L. HARRIS, *Mitchell v. Wells*

CHAPTER FOUR

Circling the Wagons and Clamping Down

The Mississippi High Court of Errors and Appeals

IN APRIL 1859 JUDGE WILLIAM L. HARRIS of the Mississippi High Court of Errors and Appeals drafted an acerbic opinion in the case of William Mitchell against Nancy Wells, one of the last cases the court would hear on the question of inheritance rights for a former slave, the biological child of her slave owner father. Judge Harris voiced the resentment felt by southerners who believed their institution of slavery was under attack in the form of free blacks liberated in northern states who then returned to their home states, claiming rights equal to whites: to sue for an inheritance. As a person born into slavery in Mississippi, Nancy Wells had no rights, and it was irrelevant in Mississippi that under Ohio law she was a free woman. Just two years prior to Fort Sumter and three years before Mississippi seceded from the Union, the court clamped down on cases such as this in an absolute rejection of precedents that had permitted cases like Nancy Wells's to be heard and relief to be granted.

Although Paul Finkelman and Mark Tushnet both discuss the case, they focus on the appellate decision and its significance as indicating either a diverging legal culture between North and South in the wake of rising abolition or as a decision indicating the perspective of the southern slave regime on interracial relationships and familial ties between owners and enslaved men and women.[1] Missing, however, is a fuller discussion of the facts of the case: Edward Wells's motivations for making a bequest to Nancy Wells, her perspectives of the events being determined by the court, and the views of others, namely beneficiaries and other witnesses to Edward Wells's lifestyle. This evidence of the facts of the case can only be found in the trial record, which I present and analyze in this chapter, in what I believe to be the first such analysis of the case.

Filing papers with the chancery court in Canton, Madison County, in August 1857 and claiming rights as a free woman of color living in Ohio, Nancy Wells hoped to receive her inheritance from William Mitchell, her cousin and the nephew of her father Edward Wells, who served as executor of the estate upon Edward's death in 1848. Mitchell refused to relinquish the $3,000, bed, and watch that Edward willed to her. Arguing that sales of various tracts of land owned by the estate could have funded her bequest, Nancy filed suit as her only recourse. She won in chancery at the trial court level in 1858, but her success was short-lived. Mitchell filed an appeal in August 1858, and the appellate court decided in his favor in 1859. Nancy did not receive the award the chancery court had granted her: $5,456.50, as calculated by the value of the property she should have received upon her father's death, plus interest and costs.[2] Instead, the decree was reversed, her bill dismissed, and she was to pay costs. A request for reargument was denied.

The opinion resulted in a spirited debate between Harris and the dissenter on the court, Alexander H. Handy. Chief Justice

Cotesworth P. Smith sided with Harris and wrote no separate opinion. As southerners with loyalties to the South, both Harris and Handy fully understood slavery's significance in their culture and supported white southerners' right to self-determination, notwithstanding growing northern sentiments against slavery. Yet the two men were not the same. Harris was born in Georgia; he lived in Columbus, Lowndes County, Mississippi, where he practiced law. He and his wife Frances had eight children, owned $10,000 in real estate, and had fourteen slaves.[3] Handy was also a lawyer, living in Madison, but he and his wife Susan had moved to the state from Maryland. They owned $5,200 in real estate and had seven children. They might not have owned any slaves.[4]

Could it be that each judge's individual histories affected how they looked at cases such as Nancy Wells's? Harris was in effect a fire-eater, a secessionist rabidly loyal to the cause: he refused to accept a position as justice to the U.S. Supreme Court in 1860 for "sectional reasons" and was a commissioner to Georgia on behalf of the secessionist cause.[5] Handy also believed in state sovereignty, serving in 1861 as a Mississippi commissioner to Maryland urging support for the secessionist cause.[6] But as his dissent indicates, he was not so fervent as to deny Nancy Wells's right to inherit as a free person of color. Moreover, by the date of the Wells decision in 1859, Handy had served longer than Harris on the bench, having joined in 1853, compared to Harris joining just the fall before.[7] Although Handy had not been on the bench for long, perhaps he developed a more nuanced jurisprudence to questions of slavery—he had seen all sorts of cases over the years and had more time to think about questions of justice and law, and the implications of decisions for state policy.

Handy accused Harris of what we would today call "legislating from the bench." At issue was the role of the judiciary in a slaveholding state: were the judges to be policy makers on the question of slavery, or were they to defer to the legislature? Was Harris formulating a new policy as a matter of judicial prerogative, or was he responding to legislative trends that had already begun earlier in the century? Handy believed that this decision to deny Nancy Wells the right to sue for an inheritance was new policy and contrary to the legislative will. As a result, he believed the court was going in an untenable direction,

Justice William L. Harris, ca. 1850. Courtesy of Mississippi Department of Archives and History.

opposing individual liberty and property rights not only for owners but for free blacks as well.

This debate over policy was at the heart of cases such as those litigated by claimants such as Nancy Wells. As a free black woman born in Mississippi but liberated by her father in Ohio, she claimed an inheritance in a slave state that had over the course of the nineteenth century curtailed the rights of free blacks living within its borders. The state legislature had early on set forth stringent requirements for owners to meet in emancipating slaves, only making those requirements more and more difficult to meet, in response to abolitionist pressure from the North and fears of free blacks living within the state. Thus slave owners of the 1820s could emancipate by last will or testament or by any other sealed writing signed before witnesses. But to effectuate the emancipation, owners were obligated "to prove to the satisfaction of the General Assembly, that such slave or slaves have done and performed some meritorious act for the benefit of such owner . . . or some distinguished service for the benefit of this state."[8] No free blacks could immigrate into the state, and each free black was obligated to register with the local authorities.[9]

But by the mid-1820s abolitionist fervor in the North was increasing, causing Mississippi legislators to pass resolutions against northern abolitionism. They also thought they were losing control in their battle to control the free black population, thus they considered even greater restrictions were necessary. In 1825 Ohio proposed a plan of gradual emancipation that would apply throughout the United States.[10] Mississippi opposed it, as it also opposed another gradual emancipation plan proposed the following year by legislatures in New Jersey, Connecticut, Indiana, and Illinois.[11] But the problems persisted unabated as not only state legislatures in the North opposed slavery, but average citizens spurred the cause. Thus, in 1836, the legislature passed a resolution asking that northern states pass penal laws against abolitionists "dangerously involving the rights, peace and domestic prosperity of this and others of the slaveholding states."[12]

A few years later in the 1830s, the legislature decided that all free blacks were to be deported: "every negro or mulatto in this State . . . shall within ninety days of this act, remove and quit the State, and shall not return within the limits of the same, under any pretense whatsoever."[13] But certain free blacks could remain: licenses could be granted to "any free negro or mulatto who shall apply . . . for permission to remain and reside in this State, and shall prove . . . that he or she is of good character and honest deportment."[14] By this time only slaves who "rendered to the state some distinguished service" could be emancipated by the legislature.[15] As for free blacks who were emancipated elsewhere but were now in Mississippi, they could be "proceeded against as a free negro or mulatto unlawfully within this State."[16] Those free blacks illegally present in the state could be brought before a justice of the peace and made to give security for good behavior; upon failure to provide security they could be imprisoned and sold into slavery.[17]

By the 1850s the legislature believed the situation had become untenable, and secession was the only answer. Northerners, they asserted, were forcing them to the brink:

We have arrived at a period in the political existence of our country . . . may ere long, be laid in ruins by the elements of discord. . . .

The fact can no longer be disguised, that our brethren of the free States . . . disregarding the compromises of the constitution . . . are determined to pursue a policy . . . destructive of [southerners'] best rights and most cherished domestic institutions.[18]

Thus Mississippi legislators met in convention with legislators of other southern states the following year, considering how they might deal with the persistent struggles over slavery.[19] Yet petitions to the legislature continued pouring in, including abolitionists' "seditious and treasonable sentiments, evincing a contemptuous disregard of the sacred guarantees of the Constitution, and evidently dictated by a blind and reckless fanaticism."[20] By joint resolution the governor was to send those resolutions back to the state officials who sent them: the governors of Maine and Vermont.

That the legislature exercised such great control over the manumission process meant that owners' initiative at the local level was limited. It also meant that Mississippi was different from other jurisdictions in which manumission petitions were heard by local courts. An owner hoping to emancipate could at most speak to a local legislator, explain his situation, and request that the legislator petition for manumission on his behalf. At that point a subcommittee comprising the legislator and about two other legislators scrutinized the evidence presented by the owner and decided whether a bill of emancipation should be granted—or the committee could simply table the petition, stalling it indefinitely. If the petition made it out of committee, it came before the entire state legislature; votes on petitions could be postponed, and petitions could be rejected outright by legislators. Although the process did not make emancipation impossible, it was arduous and protracted.

In the 1820s, just a few years after statehood, the Mississippi legislature seemed more willing to grant petitions. But by the 1830s, as the legislature began responding to greater numbers of free blacks in the state and rejected northern abolitionism, the legislature became less willing to grant them. Some petitions from the 1820s and their resolutions indicate the complexities of a manumission practice that relied upon legislative discretion. Petitioning for manumission—particularly in the case of owners seeking to manumit mixed-race slave relatives—was a delicate matter. Owners had to appeal to the legislators' sense of decency and humanity, in a regime predicated upon slaves' diminished humanity; we next examine two cases of manumission that, in the absence of other information, seem to fall into this category.

William Johnson drafted an appeal to the legislature on January 21, 1820, to manumit William, the son of an enslaved woman named Amey. He had previously manumitted her in Louisiana but did not manumit her son because the younger William had not been of age. Johnson explained that he had long lived in Mississippi, had no debts to anyone who might object to the manumission, and asked "the Honorable body to permit him to make that disposition of his property most agreeable to his feelings and consonant to humanity . . . give that Liberty to a human being which all are entitled to as a Birthright."[21] His legislator, Lewis Winston of Adams County, then submitted a petition to the House of Representatives the very next day, moving that he be a member of the subcommittee charged with deciding whether a bill would be drafted. Samuel Montgomery, also of Adams, and Harmon Runnells of Franklin, were the other members.

There is no known record of the subcommittee's deliberations. Nonetheless, about a week later on January 31, Winston presented "An act to emancipate William, a person of color."[22] That same day the bill was sent to the senate for its vote; it passed in the senate the following week, on February 5, 1820.[23] William became free. But the bill for emancipation did not pass without a struggle. A motion to postpone indefinitely was rejected by a vote of 5–3.[24]

William Johnson was able to manumit William during his lifetime, but John Morin was not as fortunate. Morin went to a justice of the peace in Hancock County to emancipate his daughter Adele and died shortly thereafter, not knowing that his action had not fulfilled the legislative requirement. His mother, Louise Favre, brought forward the petition, having realized that the emancipation of her granddaughter was invalid.

On September 8, 1821, Favre marked her affidavit because she could not write. It was then submitted to her legislator, Noel Jourdan, with the consent of her husband, Charles Favre. The affidavit stated that John Morin was her son by her late husband, Peter Morin. John purchased his eighteen-month-old daughter sometime around 1818. His purchase was contingent upon his agreement to emancipate her, a "female infant quadroon."[25] Four months afterward John Morin died intestate, asking his mother to look out for the child. But another of her sons, Peter Morin, was threatening to set aside his brother's purported act of manumission in order to keep Adele in bondage. As a result, Louise purchased the child herself from her late son's estate. Getting older in years, she worried about whether she would be able to effect John's wishes before her own death.

Unlike the Johnson case, the Morin case didn't appear to prompt a fight in the legislature on whether a bill of emancipation should be granted. On November 9, 1821, Jourdan submitted the petition, three days later reporting a bill of emancipation from the subcommittee composed of himself, Joseph Cooper, and Thomas Cotton. It was read for a second time on November 13 and for a third time on November 14. The bill passed that day as an act to emancipate Adele, "a person of color."[26] It also passed in the senate with little fanfare. Introduced on November 15, it was read again on November 16 for a third time; it then "passed with its title."[27]

It is unclear why the petitions of William Johnson and Louise Favre passed. Did the legislature perceive that the facts of the cases as presented provided ample reason to manumit? William Johnson didn't emancipate his son earlier because the boy was not of age. John Morin purchased his daughter with the intention of emancipating her, but his effort to do so pursuant to Louisiana law was undermined by a technicality. As for Louise Favre, her interest in manumission was predicated on the requirements in a bill of sale. As a result, the legislature need only regularize Johnson's manumission and accept Louise Favre's petition.

An example of an unsuccessful petition for manumission is that of Jacques Andres of Natchez. He marked his petition on December 24, 1822, stating that "divers good causes and considerations" inclined him to manumit "a certain mulatto child, of the name of Maria Louisa."[28] He didn't explain what the reasons were for his hoping to manumit her. But he provided a copy of her baptism certificate, explaining that she was the daughter of his slave Ema, born on November 18, 1820, and baptized in the Roman Catholic church in Natchez, Adams County. The petition died in committee.

The records show that three years later Andres submitted a new petition on behalf of another child he owned, Pauline, three years of age. This time he offered evidence of her merit: "That in consideration the great fidelity already manifested towards him on the part of said child and being unwilling that she should remain in slavery during life."[29] Whatever his motivation in stating his reasons, his representative in the house, Charles B. Green, brought forth the petition in January 1824. He made up the select committee with Representatives Merry Bracy and Joseph McAfee. Green presented a bill of manumission on January 6. The bill was read again on January 9, when a motion by William Haile of Wilkinson County to postpone the bill indefinitely was voted down. On the second reading later that day Haile tried again, to no avail. Two days later, however, the "act to manumit Pauline, a slave of Jacque Andres," failed by a vote of 18–14.[30]

Haile's persistence in defeating Jacques Andres's 1823 petition to manumit Pauline may find reason in some of his activities around that time. In January he was on a select committee to which was referred a resolution sent to the governor of Mississippi from the legislatures of New Jersey, Connecticut, Delaware, Indiana, and Illinois. They were seeking a gradual emancipation bill. Haile read the committee's response on January 9:

> Under the constitution and laws of our country, the right of property in slaves, is as sacred and inviolable, as that of any other species of personal property whatever—However great, may be the national evil of slavery, and however much, we may regret it, circumstances over which we could have no control, have rendered it inevitable, and places it without the pale of Legislative authority. We therefore, cannot concur in any arrangement for their emancipation, by any Legislative enactment, without violating the constitutional rights of our citizens.[31]

Perhaps Haile perceived granting emancipation petitions would be a dangerous policy in light of northern abolitionist pressure. It could

be seen as sending the message that the legislature was not fully pro-
tective of the institution of slavery in the state, by contributing to the
numbers of free blacks.

As a result of these tensions, what had been contentious in the late
1820s would become rancorous by the 1830s. In at least two cases
from 1833, legislators were absolutely unwilling to hear manumission
petitions in which slave owners might have been seeking to manumit
biological enslaved children: the Collins petition and a petition on
behalf of the late Benjamin Nail.

On February 26, 1833, Alexander Morrison of Hinds County presented the petition of Jane Collins and others who sought to manumit two enslaved children. It was explained that "Timothy Terrell
died after making his last will and testament" and that "he desired
that two mulatto children, born slaves . . . should be emancipated
upon arriving of lawful age." The children, named Eliza and Charles,
born of an enslaved woman named Patty, were just of the age to
be manumitted, and Jane Collins's petition set out why the matter
was important: "your petitioners are desirous that the human and
benevolent intentions of said testator may be carried into effect. . . .
[T]hey do not feel themselves authorised to hold said mulattos in
slavery nor do they believe that any public detriment or evil conse-
quence will result."[32]

Immediately after Morrison presented the petition, and before he
had read it, Philip Dixon of Jefferson made a motion to table it;
the motion passed. Morrison's subsequent request to withdraw the
petition was denied. Upon a motion from the chair, Joseph Dunbar,
Morrison was ordered to withdraw the documents accompanying the
petition.[33] The other legislators prevented Morrison from providing
context for the matter at hand and certainly prevented Jane Collins's
reasons from being heard in the legislature. It could be said that
their actions to muzzle Morrison made it easier for them to remain
focused upon abstract policy: reinforcement of slavery and denial of
manumission. With that move, the petition was tabled.

Something similar happened later that year on the second reading of the bill to manumit Delila, a slave owned by the late Benjamin
Nail. Nathan Rea, Nail's executor, gave Tilghman Tucker of Lowndes
a petition to manumit. As was typical, Tucker chaired the subcommit-

tee. In his will Nail stated he wanted to liberate Delila for her honorable and faithful service. On December 9 Tucker presented the committee's recommended bill of manumission, without incident.[34] But on December 14, when the bill was read again, William Van Norman of Amite moved that it be indefinitely postponed, at which point Tucker called for a reading of the supporting documents to the petition: the will and affidavits presented by Rea. But "the House refused to sustain the call," and Samuel L. Gholson of Monroe moved that Tucker be excused from voting on the question of whether the bill should be indefinitely postponed. The resolution passed. Eighteen members voted that the bill be indefinitely postponed, and six voted against.[35]

By now the trend was clear: not only could petitions for manumission be rejected, but legislators who dared bring them on behalf of constituents might be rebuffed. This was a message to be broadcast within the house, as members saw what could happen to legislators who supported manumission requests. As counseled, it was the message legislators would have given to constituents who brought such requests. Rejection of petitions and humiliation of legislators could have fueled the push to manumit outside of the state.

The hostile environment in the House of Representatives didn't mean that no petitions were granted during the 1830s and into the 1840s, as demonstrated by the cases of Littleton Tyson, David Holmes, and Israel Loring. In the first case, Littleton Tyson ordered and directed in his last will and testament that a female slave named Leathy should be manumitted. Because she gave "evidence of good character," the legislature ordered her emancipated and set free. But she was also to give bond and security that she would "never become a public charge, and . . . [maintain] good behavior."[36] As for two slaves of the late governor David Holmes, the legislature was effusive about emancipating Lewis and Nancy: "whereas the legislature and the people . . . entertain the most lively regard for the memory of the deceased . . . and whereas it appears . . . the said negroes sustain a good character," the two slaves became free. They were to provide bond and security.[37]

Israel Loring of Claiborne County intended that his slaves Peter, his wife Sucky (also Suckey), and their daughter Fanny become free upon his death. In his will, he stated they were to receive a plot of land, money, livestock, and one year's worth of provisions. If it proved difficult to manumit them in the state they were to be manumitted elsewhere, and if they decided to go to Liberia they would receive $350 in cash instead. It is unclear whether they ever received the full bequest Loring intended they receive. But the legislature permitted them to remain in Port Gibson, where they lived. In an interesting twist, the executors, rather than the individuals to be freed, were to provide bond, "conditioned for the orderly conduct and good behaviour of the said Peter, Suckey, and Fanny, and that they shall not become a public charge."[38]

This bond requirement was significant insofar as the legislature put into place during the 1820s requirements that must be met by all free blacks found in Mississippi, not just those newly manumitted, in an effort to clamp down on free blacks illegally in the state: registration of free blacks lawfully in the state, expulsion, and possible reenslavement of those with no lawful presence. This new registration requirement generated anxieties in the free black community. Thus, various white community members who knew Esther Barland of Adams County filed a petition on her behalf. Legislative provisions in the act of 1822 threatened her ability to remain in Mississippi. They hoped she might be granted permission to remain. It was granted, and a resolution passed by the legislature stated that she could remain, provided that she too fulfill the bond requirement and "demean herself exemplary in every respect."[39]

Although nothing in the statute specifically indicates a definition of good behavior, we can presume it focused on hard work and abstemiousness. Since many whites believed that free blacks degenerated into indolence and crime without the civilizing influences of white control through enslavement, free blacks had to prove their industry lest they become incapable of supporting themselves. If free persons were no longer self-supporting, they became public charges, and the bond was to protect the local authorities from having to provide for their upkeep.

In a society in which maintaining racial hierarchy was crucial, it would also have been important that free blacks avoid behavior that might infer arrogance, such as that the free black person thinking himself or herself socially or politically equal to whites. Insolence was a deadly sin in the eyes of owners, insofar as free blacks privileged with rights to work for wages and travel freely could provide a dangerous example to those blacks who were still enslaved. This perception of free blacks lay at the heart of white objection to an increase in their population in the state. Whites feared that free blacks were capable of starting insurrection, and in the particular case of mixed-race blacks whose petitions to remain in the state were considered by the legislature, their ties to whites made them even more dangerous. These free blacks had white fathers and allies within the white community who could provide them even greater means to empower themselves: money and other resources.

Esther Barland, in all likelihood, was part of an established mixed-race family. Various members of the Barland family had gained their freedom during Mississippi's territorial days, when William Barland of Adams County gained permission from the legislative council and the House of Representatives in 1814 to manumit thirteen persons of color: "a female named and commonly called Elizabeth and her twelve children, and the acknowledged children of him the said William Barland."[40] The children's names were Andrew, Elizabeth, Margaret, James, William Jr., Adam, David, George, Alexander, John, Agnes, and Susanna. Their manumission was contingent upon William Sr. providing a $10,000 bond that no one in his family would become a public charge.

But this freedom placed them in a precarious position, nonetheless. Andrew Barland later tried to no avail to obtain the privileges of whiteness, that is, to testify in court. His testimony in a legal dispute had been challenged because of his race. It is unclear whether his legal rights in the dispute were at stake; nonetheless, he argued that although he was born of a white man and a mixed-race black woman, he had been raised as a white man. As a result he deserved the same privileges. He had been well educated, married a white woman, and owned land and slaves.[41] Yet his rights could still be compromised. His ability to testify could be questioned because, as was explained by Thomas Cobb, the writer of a treatise on slavery: "The freed negro does not become a citizen by virtue of his manumission. It requires the act of another party, the State, to clothe him with civil and political rights."[42] This was something the legislature was not willing to do — remove the disabilities of race.

Esther Barland was also worried about her rights as a free woman of color living in Mississippi. Had something happened in the eight-year period between the passage of the registration act of 1822 and the time the resolution in her favor was passed in 1830? Had her right to remain in the state been challenged? Perhaps she had no proof of her freeborn status, insofar as the legislature required free blacks to explain whether they had been born free, freed by last will and testament, or freed by other written instrument. On the other hand, perhaps the petition was her insurance policy against future problems. She had proof from the legislature that she was a free woman of color.

By the 1830s and 1840s then, the legislature was placing free blacks under greater scrutiny; at the same time the older legislative practice of deferring to owners' prerogatives to manumit had fallen into disfavor. These changes happened to the misfortune of some owners who hoped to manumit in this period, and to the detriment of their slave beneficiaries. This new legislative approach was wary of manumission in the state and also increased the burden of proof for owners before manumission could be granted, fueling the push for them to manumit outside of the state's borders. This became particularly apparent after the high threshold of "distinguished service" to the state was implemented. The owner of a favored slave, his biological child, could not meet such a standard, since his affection for his child was not grounded in the child's service to the state. It was a standard Edward Wells couldn't meet; as a result, he took Nancy to Ohio.

Although the legislature never barred free blacks from suing in the state, Harris argued that in the case of Nancy Wells, precedent should be overturned as a matter of public policy. In Harris's view no free black had any right to sue in Mississippi, even though individual rights, long the hallmark of Anglo-American jurisprudence, were at stake. For example, the legislature since 1822 had provisions in place to protect free blacks who alleged they were being "illegally detained as a slave in the possession of another."[43] They could petition the local circuit court for their freedom. But for Harris in 1859, societal needs were more important: protection of slavery's hierarchy. Free blacks placed that system of hierarchy in jeopardy.

The case of *Hinds v. Brazealle*, precedent from a few decades before, set the tone for Harris's opinion.[44] Elisha Brazealle took his enslaved partner and their son John Monroe Brazealle to Ohio in 1826. He gave them deeds of emancipation. He then returned with them to his home in Jefferson County, where they all lived until his death. Acknowledging John Brazealle as his son, Elisha Brazealle "recited the fact that he had executed a deed of emancipation, declared his intentions to ratify said deed," and left John all his estate.[45] The court found that Elisha Brazealle did not pursue the proper channels and aimed to circumvent the strict requirements of the law, therefore his strategy to manumit and grant property was in violation of Mississippi law and policy:

> Free negroes are deemed offensive, because they are not permitted to emigrate to, or remain in the state. . . . They are required to leave the state within thirty days after notice, and in the meantime give security for good behavior, and those of them who can lawfully remain, must register and carry with them their certificates, or they may be committed to jail. . . . No owner can emancipate his slave, but by a deed or will properly attested, or acknowledged in court, and proof to the legislature, that such slave has performed some meritorious act for the benefit of the owner . . . or the state. . . . [T]he deed or will can have no validity unless ratified by special act of the legislature.[46]

The attempted manumission was thus voided; John Brazealle and his mother were slaves to be divided up among the heirs at law.

For white testator fathers who manumitted their partners and children elsewhere and liquidated their estates in Mississippi, the most recent precedent had been decided by the court only a year prior to its decision in the Wells case, *Shaw v. Brown* (Miss., 1858), and the facts of this older case were similar.[47] James Brown of Amite County had taken his mulatto sons Francis and Jerome to Cincinnati, Ohio, for the purpose of manumitting them. He then set them up to live with their slave mother Harriet in Indiana. James Brown returned to Mississippi, but his family did not. Thereafter, he made a will stating that the entire estate should be liquidated, all the debts be paid, and the remainder deposited in a Louisiana bank. The court decided in favor of the will, rejecting the challenge of John Brown, James's brother. Handy wrote the opinion, explaining that the manumission and grant of inheritance was legitimate and valid. James Brown was within his rights to manumit his family outside of the state, and their inheritance rights did not in any way affect slavery in Mississippi. They need not ever live in the state as freed people, but were living elsewhere.

Arguably, Nancy Wells was also of no threat to slavery in Mississippi. She had not been manumitted in Mississippi, and she need never live in Mississippi as a free person, since she filed her action as a resident of Cincinnati, Ohio. The chancery court gave her a cash award, and she need not return to the state in order to receive it. Why then did the court later reject this most recent precedent? Within a year after the decision in *Shaw v. Brown*, Harris was on the court, and he brought with him his totally different perspective. A speech he gave in November, a month after his election to the high court, foreshadowed his sentiments.

In addressing the state agricultural association, he proposed that Mississippians develop local industry and patronize local merchants, in an effort to keep wealth in the state, away from "the skinny fingers of every heartless vendor, or pedlar of worthless trumpery from abolition land, who gambles . . . that he may reap the gains of his avaricious venture."[48] He claimed that northern merchants cultivated greed and preyed upon southerners' demand for luxury goods, only making southerners vulnerable in the end, because while states like Mississippi cultivated cotton, northerners were the source of manufactured goods. To rely so much on northerners was dangerous, he asserted; the times were perilous, and independence was called for:

> We have long been advised by the action of the North . . . when we are daily and hourly warned by the continued disregard of our wants, our rights, and their constitutional obligations; when the voices of half the States of this Union . . . are heard in concert, threatening the institution of slavery, and a dissolution of the Union. . . . When conventions of Free-negroes are openly permit-

ted and countenanced in sister States, defying the constitution and laws of the land . . . the importance of State action looking to independence at home as a measure of safety, becomes immeasurably enhanced.[49]

Five months afterward the court heard Nancy Wells's case, and it evoked all of Harris's resentment of northerners and their disrespect for the southern institution of slavery. Wells wrote in her complaint that she was a free woman of color about twenty years of age, the daughter of Edward Wells, a single man never married to a white wife, and "a Planter of great wealth [who] owned slaves, among others the Mother of the said Nancy your oratrix."[50] Edward had taken her to Ohio in 1846, liberated her there "and placed her for education with one Hiram Gilmore, who then was principal of a school in Cincinnati kept principally for the education of colored youth."[51]

Around August 8, 1846, after she had been in Cincinnati a week, her father visited her at the house where she was boarding. She was measured and her features noted, for the purpose of preparing a certificate of manumission: "five feet two or three inches in height . . . a bright mulatto woman with black hair nearly straight has in the left side of her cheek near the lower part of nostril a large black mole and a scar just blow [*sic*] her hair on the top of her forehead running obliquely along the line of her hair."[52] She remained in Ohio for two years, with her father's permission. She was not treated as a slave, and no one made any demand that she return to slavery in Mississippi. Although she did not have a copy of a certificate of manumission, her attorneys Jolliffe and Gitchell sued to have her declared a free woman of color. Pursuant to order of the Court of Common Pleas, Hamilton County, she was a free woman.

That court order establishing Nancy Wells's freedom clothed her with rights to sue for an inheritance. Her cousin William Mitchell and various relatives, she claimed, divided up the property pursuant to the will, taking their shares but disregarding her interests. She was a free woman of color, Edward Wells having recognized her rights pursuant to the second clause of his will: "I leave to Nancy Wells a Mulatto Girl about eighteen years of age whom I have raised and liberated, the sum of three thousand dollars to be raised from the sale of my property, also the silver Watch worn by me, also my feather Bed."[53] Although Edward never explicitly called her his daughter in his will, people understood her to be. Patrick Henry, who wrote the will, explained that Edward was Nancy's father and he had every intention of ensuring she became a free woman and leaving her a legacy.[54]

Although Edward Wells was solicitous of her welfare, naming her in his will and sending her to Jackson, Mississippi, to learn the dressmaking trade, as Hannah Dudley testified, that did not mean that she was especially privileged. Edward Wells visited Dudley sometime in 1847 or 1848, before he died, "to know whether I would not take a colored girl to learn the Dress making business."[55] Her unwillingness led Edward to bargain with her on his daughter's behalf: "He then said that she was a free girl and that he wished her to learn the business of Dressmaking in order that she could support herself in a free state Where he intended to send her."[56] She recalled his persistence and that he "held out inducements for me to do so by stating that she could do housework for me and any light housework not Drudging. I then agreed that she might come with the understanding that she was to do light housework about the House and to sew when she had time."[57]

Alan Taylor lived briefly at the Wells house in 1847 while Nancy was away at school, and was living there when she returned to live in Mississippi—Edward had found it too expensive to maintain her in Ohio. During Taylor's time at the household he observed that she didn't appear to be treated as a slave but "in the place of a servant about the House of Wells. . . . I never saw her working in the field."[58] But her mother, unnamed in court documents, might have been a fieldworker. The mother's slave status meant that Edward Wells could separate the two and establish himself as Nancy's sole parent, according to Francis A. Mitchell, William Mitchell's wife: "[Edward] Wells said that Nancy['s] Mother had ill treated her, and that he had sold her Mother while the child was very small[;] he retained the child that she had been raised about his house and that he was attached to her."[59]

All this testimony gave credence to Nancy's rights as her father's legitimate heir. But William Mitchell denied all of Nancy Wells's claims, replying to the chancery court complaint: "This Court cannot take Jurisdiction of the said pretended complainant and of her Bill of complaint nor grant her any relief thereon, because the said pretended complainant is a Negro slave of African descent and the Offspring of a slave of African descent."[60] William Mitchell knew the terms of the will and that Nancy Wells was listed as a beneficiary, and it is noteworthy that, despite having pledged as executor to fulfill the testator's wishes to the best of his ability and to undertake legal obligations to do so, he did not renounce and refuse to serve. This would have absolved him of responsibility for fulfilling the terms of the will. Instead he put himself in the position of having to face a lawsuit and answer for his refusal to provide the bequests: "the pretended complainant is not now and never was 'a free woman of color' . . . nor does he admit complainant was the Daughter of said Wells."[61] He admitted, nonetheless, that there were clauses in the will that referred to Nancy Wells, including a codicil that instructed the executors to invest the money on her behalf.

A question that arises on close examination of the case is whether William Mitchell always intended to violate Edward Wells's trust. He lived with his wife in the Wells house during his lifetime, both knew of Edward's affairs, and as a result Edward must have trusted Mitchell to fulfill his wishes. He knew Nancy was Edward's daughter and a free woman of color. His wife knew that Edward took Nancy to Ohio because getting a legislative bill of manumission in Mississippi had become impossible. According to her, William Mitchell accompanied Edward in bringing Nancy to learn dressmaking from Hannah Dudley in Jackson.[62] Mitchell himself had been present at her wedding to a barber, Sam Watts. John R. Lambeth, the Methodist Episcopal minister who officiated at the 1848 ceremony, a short time prior to Edward's death, explained "there was a conversation between William Mitchell and myself. . . . Mitchell said she was free or was about to be free."[63] Edward agreed to the wedding and would permit his daughter to marry only on proof that her fiancé was a free man of color. After visiting the newlyweds in their home in Jackson in October 1848, Edward chatted with Francis Mitchell, as she reported "expressed himself very well pleased, saying that they were very well settled and fixed for Housekeeping, and said if I would occasionally send them a few articles from the plantation they would do very well."[64]

An important point in this case is that Nancy Wells claimed that she became imperiled the moment she began fighting for her inheritance. Francis Mitchell explained: "Nancy was informed that she could be legally claimed by the heirs of Edward Wells as a slave belonging to his estate. I was informed that she ran away to prevent being sold as a part of the Estate."[65] In fact Francis was the one who told Nancy that her situation was precarious. Thus Nancy Wells left "without the consent of the Defendant [William Mitchell,] Who had the legal control of the said Wells estate."[66] In the eyes of her cousin, she was not a beneficiary but part of the bounty to be divided up.

Judge Harris did not address the question of whether Nancy Wells should be considered part of the estate, but he explained clearly that as a woman born into slavery in Mississippi she had no right to bring suit in Mississippi, and thus no rights to an inheritance. He prefaced his decision with a discussion that the case demanded a measure of policy making on the part of the judiciary: "in great questions of public policy . . . involving the security of our institutions and the safety of the people, I do not feel that I am at liberty . . . to yield my convictions of duty and official responsibility . . . however well established in matters of private right."[67]

Nancy Wells never had any rights as a free woman of color in Mississippi, because, as asserted in the *Mitchell v. Wells* decision, "a slave, once domiciliated as such, in this State, can acquire no right, civil or political, by manumission elsewhere."[68] As for *Shaw v. Brown*, it was irrelevant to Harris that the court recently found that "when slaves are taken out of this State to a free State, with the intent to emancipate them, and bring them back into this State, *if they are not so brought back, such emancipation* is not against the policy of our laws, and is not void *in the State of Mississippi*" (original emphasis).[69] In the court's earlier view it was "not against the policy of this State that free negroes of other States should exercise, in this State, all rights secured to them by the laws of other States where they are domiciled, so far as they are not positively prohibited, or are not dangerous to the condition of our slaves."[70]

All that was irrelevant, in Harris's view: "comity [as a matter of one state respecting the judgments and orders of another] is subordinate to sovereignty, and cannot, therefore, contravene our public policy, or the rights, interests, or safety of our State or people."[71] As Finkelman noted in *Imperfect Union,* once northern jurisdictions began recognizing the formerly enslaved as free people of color with rights, southerners grew resentful and less willing to recognize the rights of these former slaves in their home jurisdictions. Thus, Harris explained, Mississippi opposed all manumissions, not just "*the increase of free negroes in this State*" (original emphasis), and as such, it should not be forced to recognize manumissions taking place in Ohio or elsewhere, particularly when an act of 1857 banned slave owners from manumitting slaves within the state or elsewhere:

> Nor shall it be lawful for any executor . . . or other person . . . to remove any slave or slaves from this State, with the intent to emancipate such slave or slaves. . . . all such wills, deeds . . . or other arrangements . . . intended to accomplish the emancipation . . . no matter when made, shall be deemed and held entirely null and void.[72]

Reading this most recent statute, Harris believed as a matter of Mississippi law and policy that manumissions should not be encouraged and a free woman of color like Nancy Wells should be barred from asserting any right to inherit in Mississippi.

But perhaps Harris's reading of precedent and legislation was overly broad, and not sufficiently tailored to the facts at hand. Nancy Wells was never prosecuted or found guilty of being in the state illegally. She returned to Mississippi around 1848 after being manumitted in Ohio in 1846, with the full consent of her slave owner father, and no one, including William Mitchell, protested. By the time she brought her action she was living in Cincinnati again. Finally, nothing in the will of Edward Wells purported to manumit her, thus making the 1857 act irrelevant. She was not a slave under his 1848 will, having been manumitted two years prior, and she was thus not to be passed along as property to the other heirs. Instead, she was a free woman of color whose rights Harris did not believe need be respected.

This sentiment is reminiscent of *Scott v. Sandford,* in which Chief Justice Taney of the U.S. Supreme Court wrote an 1857 opinion two years prior to Harris's decision in *Mitchell v. Wells*, in an attempt to end forever all discussion of whether slaves had rights to freedom based upon domicile in a free state.[73] Harris found Taney's decision inspirational:

Negroes whose ancestors were imported into the United States and sold as slaves "are not included, and were not intended to be included under the word 'citizens' in the Constitution of the United States, and can therefore claim none of the rights and privileges which that instrument provides for and secures to the citizens of the United States. On the contrary, they were, at that time, considered a subordinate and inferior class of beings, who had been subjugated by the dominant race, and whether emancipated or not, yet remained subject to their authority, and had no rights or privileges but such as those who held the power and the Government might choose to grant them."[74]

Nancy Wells was thus entitled only to the rights Mississippi chose to give her, which rights, as far as Harris was concerned, did not exist. She had no rights that anyone was bound to consider under law, meaning that her cousin William Mitchell, as executor of his uncle Edward Wells's will, was free to ignore the bequest left her, and the court was thus free to overturn the decision of the chancellor, E. G. Henry, who granted her bequest. It also meant that Edward Wells, as a white man, also had no rights that Mitchell was bound to respect. For although Nancy Wells brought a lawsuit challenging Mitchell's behavior, her cause of action grew out of Edward Wells's last wishes. And even though Harris recognized that individual rights were at stake, those individual rights and last wishes were irrelevant in the face of state policies that opposed the manumission of free blacks.

This is significant because they did not recognize the case to be about familial relationships: the moral obligation Edward Wells believed he had to his mixed-race enslaved daughter and the denial of familial relationship on the part of her cousin, William Mitchell. Did they fail to address individual rights in light of parental obligations because although Edward treated Nancy as his daughter, and others knew he was her purported father, nowhere in the will did he name her as such? His behavior spoke for him, and in his dealings with others he was clear about their relationship. However, in this official document, his will, he only described her as a mulatto girl he raised. Perhaps because Edward Wells was oblique it gave Harris and the other judges room to treat the matter as an abstract one over the rights of a free woman of color to sue in Mississippi for property she believed she was entitled to.

Handy replied that contrary to Harris's view, "the abstract policy of slavery, or of the manumission or freedom of slaves, is a question not belonging to this forum, nor proper to be determined by it."[75] The simple question to be determined by the court was "*to adjudicate* whether an emancipated slave has certain legal rights claimed by her" (original emphasis).[76] In his view Harris misread the act of 1842 as opposing all manumissions altogether, because he ignored "the positive recognition of the right of the owner to take his slave to another State and manumit him there, contained in the second section."[77] Handy argued forcefully that the court was improperly inserting itself into legislative matters:

> *To declare a policy* for the State which the legislature . . . has not established, and which is firmly settled . . . not to be within the policy established by the legislature; thus unsettling the law of this court upon the subject, and arrogating to the court the powers of the legislature . . . must prostrate the character and usefulness of the court, by rendering the rules held by it fluctuating and uncertain . . . no one can feel secure in the rights which he has acquired. . . . All security for private right is destroyed. . . . *The individual opinions of the judges,* for the time being, and not *the law as settled,* become the rule of action. The conservative character of the court is broken down, and all confidence in the stability of its rules is destroyed in the minds of good citizens. [all original emphasis][78]

Harris was politicizing the court's adjudications, an improper judicial response to national tensions over abolition. Granted, Handy was no abolitionist, and he favored slavery as a matter of domestic law internal to Mississippi, but he argued, "We have no right to complain of, the internal policy of a sovereign State . . . in allowing rights to a free person of color, though we may and do think that policy is wrong in principle and dangerous in practice."[79] However, he realized that Harris's opinion developed out of a southern response to northerners opposing the repatriation of fugitives. Southerners were engaging in a game of "tit-for-tat," that as a result of abolitionist policies, southerners were right in denying "claim[s] to international comity in reference to the rights of free negroes who may seek to assert rights in our courts."[80] Instead, Handy believed Mississippi should "respect and enforce the rights of residents of other States."[81] As long as the United States existed as an entity, comity should be respected.

Handy realized that comity was important in these cases because of the ways in which free blacks were vulnerable to the machinations of unscrupulous whites. Just a few years prior, Handy wrote an opinion in *Leiper v. Hoffman et al.* (Miss., 1853) in which Fanny Leiper, a free woman of color from Natchez, purchased a vacant lot in 1834 for $175 and spent $1,500 to build a house on the property. She lived there, paying for everything, including assessments and property taxes, until May 1845, when she moved to Cincinnati, Ohio. She had Samuel R. Hammitt act as her agent to lease the property and manage it on her behalf. Because she was concerned that "there was a great spirit at the time to remove from the State all free persons of color," her attorney advised her to put the deed in her name and the name of a trustworthy white person.[82] In 1836 Joseph Winscott of New Orleans was listed as co-owner.

Thereafter, a neighbor, Malvina Hoffman, told Winscott that according to her understanding of the situation, Leiper was a slave and not a free person of color. As a result, he owned the property in the entirety because as a slave Leiper could own no property under the law. This woman then obtained the property fraudulently, purchasing it from Winscott for $100 on September 27, 1845. In his answer to the court, Winscott claimed that all the property was his and that he was justified in selling it, since he said he had paid for everything and had put Leiper's name on the deed "merely to gratify a whim on her part."[83] This comprised Hoffman and Winscott's defense to Leiper's claim.

Leiper did not learn of the fraud until a month after the sale. As a result, she brought suit against both Hoffman and Winscott to have the deed of sale canceled, the title put into her name only, and for an accounting of rents and any damages to the property. Although the chancery court held in favor of the defendants, Leiper won a reversal on appeal. Handy wrote in criticism of Winscott and Hoffman's defrauding behavior and perjurious testimony: "While the complainant resided in Natchez . . . no effort seems to have been made to disturb her ownership of the property. But shortly after her removal to Ohio, the defendant Hoffman appears to have entertained the idea of acquiring it."[84] He was highly critical of Winscott's "conduct . . . as it appears through his answer," which he found didn't entitle him "to favorable consideration in a court of equity, as in good morals," adding also that Hoffman's behavior was not "much more commendable."[85]

Handy's opinion in *Leiper v. Hoffman et al.* informs Handy's discussion of the ramifications of the court's holding in *Mitchell v. Wells*: "Suppose a free negro of another state is abducted and brought into this state, and held in slavery, or his property is taken . . . or a right belonging to him in this State is withheld, has he no remedy for such a wrong?"[86] Indeed this is what had happened to Nancy Wells: a right that she argued belonged to her had been withheld. What if she had been kidnapped from Ohio, where she was living, and brought back to Mississippi or taken elsewhere? Francis Mitchell testified that the other heirs to the estate wanted to claim her as part of the property, and Nancy Wells asserted in her complaint that she might be at risk of being kidnapped. She alleged that William Mitchell sent a letter to her in Ohio dated May 27, 1855, about two years prior to her filing suit, in which he is purported to have said:

> I am traveling with my family to spend the summer in Kentucky and Virginia. . . . I have written to you by mail several time [*sic*] in the last two years, and have not got an answer from you. I wish you would write to me and direct your letter to Frankfort Kentucky . . . and let me know if you can come there to see me in August. . . . I am very anxious to settle my business with you and I cannot agree to do it with any one but yourself. . . . If you can come let me know

and I will meet you in Frankfort. . . . I am anxious that you should do well and have a good support in Cincinnati. . . . I am a friend to you as you will find—though some people tried to make you believe I am not your friend.[87]

Mitchell claimed the letter was fraudulent. But what if it wasn't and the allegations she made in her complaint were true? What if as a result of Nancy Wells's dealings with her cousin Mitchell she was afraid he "might cause her to be arrested and taken from and out of the state of Ohio, to parts wholly unknown to her and to do her some other and utter and irreparable infamy"?[88] Frankfort was the capital of Kentucky, a slave state. According to Nancy, Mitchell was suggesting she leave Cincinnati, accompanied by no one, and meet with him in Frankfort. She feared what might happen to her, including Mitchell selling her into slavery or charging her with being a fugitive slave. The fugitive slave act had just been passed in 1850, making it easier for owners to claim persons they believed to be runaway slaves. Using Harris's logic, if Nancy Wells's worst fears had been realized she would have had no recourse, even though the act of 1857 included specific provisions to be used by free persons of color held illegally in slavery.[89] As far as Harris was concerned, a free black woman had no right to access the courts in Mississippi.

We can only surmise what happened to Nancy Wells. We do know that on June 4, 1860, census enumerators appeared in Cincinnati's Fifteenth Ward. Thomas Colston, a black man from Virginia, was the head of a household that included his wife Margaret and three children born in Ohio. Living with them was a twenty-eight-year-old black woman, also listed as being from Virginia: Nancy Watts, a seamstress.[90] The name—Watts was Nancy's married name—and the description matched that of Nancy Wells, except for the place of birth. Did the census enumerator make a mistake in describing her as being from Virginia? A year after the Mississippi High Court of Errors and Appeals decided her case, was she still trying to hide, fearful of being kidnapped, but working as a seamstress? If the woman enumerated in the census was Nancy Wells, although she did not receive her inheritance, she had learned the trade of dressmaking that her father made sure she gained in order that she might make her way in the world.

Nancy Wells's decision to flee was a shrewd response to policy developments, and it was predicated on the significance of geography. Her father had her manumitted in Ohio once manumission in Mississippi became more difficult, and she lived there for two years in the 1840s. While living there she developed and cultivated relationships within the community of free blacks who could provide her support when she needed to run for her life and hide. The Mississippi High Court of Errors and Appeals had already denied the free status of former slaves manumitted out of the state who then returned to Mississippi. Even if she had remained in Mississippi, defended her right to freedom, and won, she might have still been forced to leave, for free blacks manumitted in the 1850s could be forced to emigrate, as in the case of a woman named Mary.

Thomas Y. Gwinstead of Lawrence County manumitted Mary and her five children — Francis, James, Henry, Louisa, and Martha — pursuant to his will. The legislature assented to the manumission: "provided that they shall be removed within one year after the passage of this act, by the executor or trustee under said will."[91] Without the right to remain in the state, and the legislature becoming more and more hostile to the free blacks who remained, what happened to those forced to flee but who had nowhere to go, or who had significant personal ties they didn't want to lose? By 1860 the answer was reenslavement.

A few months before the census takers jotted down Nancy Wells's information, the legislature passed an act that made William Webster, a free man of color from Tallahatchie, the slave of Atherald Ball. Perhaps he had been faced with expulsion and concluded that his safest bet was to become the slave of a trusted white person and hope for the best: connection with family, friends, and community. With his new status, he became "a slave for life," upon Ball agreeing to become his owner.[92] This could just as easily have been Nancy Wells's fate: reenslavement and loss of freedom. Her white relatives would have been more than willing to serve as her new owners.

We the undersigned citizens of the State of South Carolina, humbly
petition your honourable body's [*sic*] to take into consideration the fact
that white men in this community are frequently found living in open
connection with negro and mulatto women, in a manner disreputable to
the neighborhood in which they reside, setting a pernicious example to
our youth, and assailing the institutions of slavery through the process
of a tolerated amalgamation. We therefore suggest to your Honourable
bodies that you make it by enactment at this Session of the Legislature
an indictable offense for any white man, resident in this state, to live in
open connection with a negro or mulatto woman, as his wife, whether
married or unmarried.

—Petition to the state legislature from the men of Barnwell, 1860

CHAPTER FIVE

The People of Barnwell against the Supreme Court of South Carolina

The Case of Elijah Willis

STATE MANUMISSION POLICIES that permitted free blacks to live
within the state drew white citizens into legislative debates, insofar as they used petitions to state their preference. As indicated in
Mississippi, local whites signed affidavits in support of the manumission of local blacks. Others signed petitions in support of policies
that would deny their neighbors the right to remain in the state.
But in South Carolina the struggle over inheritance rights for slave
partners and their children pushed local whites to petition the legislature to reject a decision signed by the state high court in upholding

the will of an elite white man who left a large estate in real and personal property. Elijah Willis, introduced in chapter 1, gave the bulk of his property to an enslaved woman named Amy and her children. Men in the community were angered over what upholding such wills might mean: subversion of the system of slavery and loss of white wealth.

In the spring of 1860 fifty white men of Barnwell, South Carolina, signed a petition to the state legislature signaling their resistance to miscegenation and seeking a remedy the law courts could not offer. Titled "Petition of Sundry Citizens of Barnwell Praying Further Legislation in reference to colored population," the petition actually sought control over white men: it called for a law that would enable the punishment of white men found to be living openly with black women.[1]

These planters, merchants, and lawyers were protesting the limitations of judicial decision making. For in that term the Supreme Court of South Carolina heard the final appeal of a will contest that had begun five years before, when Elijah Willis, a local landowner and planter, brought his enslaved partner Amy, her mother, and seven children to Ohio, only to die there and leave a will granting them a substantial estate of real and personal property. Willis was in his sixties and unmarried; Amy was in her early thirties. He had, however, heirs at law, that is, legitimate white relatives—his siblings and their children—who contested the will and sought to nullify the bequests.

Contrary to the demands of a slave regime predicated on strict legal boundaries between owner and slave and the retention of property in the interests of whiteness, the high court, led by Justice John Belton O'Neall, held that Amy and the others were entitled to receive the property because they were no longer slaves (*Willis v. Jolliffe*, 1860). The will drafted in Ohio was ruled valid, and the challengers were not entitled to the whole. By bringing the nine to Ohio, Willis ensured their freedom and their ability to receive the bequests. The men who signed the petition and sent it to the legislature thus marked their protest in response, as opposing miscegenation.

Willis traveled from South Carolina to Ohio, only to die unexpectedly and dramatically on his arrival.[2] At the time he was with his traveling companions—the enslaved woman Amy, her children, and mother—and a will on his person was one he had made in Ohio the previous year. But another will made in South Carolina years before was different in every way. The earlier will left his property to his siblings and their spouses. The later one gave all to Amy and the children. After the case was resolved, local community members filed a petition protesting the resolution of this case of conflicting wills, the petition that is the epigraph for this chapter.

The case of Elijah Willis indicates struggles within an ethos of slavery and community. The law of slavery empowered whites, but these fifty men did not feel that existing societal institutions were adequate to control those who transgressed racial boundaries, and they used a unique approach: the right to petition government as the basis of American political freedoms. Perhaps fears of an increasing enslaved and free black population empowered through access to whiteness underlay their fears, and they saw their petition as the only means left to them to prevent white wealth from slipping into the hands of slaves. Not only did the petition indicate the men's fears of social upheaval, but it demonstrated the men's resistance to law as formulated by the courts. The court's decision opposed the interests of the community; thus, the fifty sought legislative redress to protect white supremacy: a pure white race, and the retention of white wealth.

In the rural, inland community of Barnwell the enslaved population exceeded the local population. In 1860 there were 12,702 whites living in Barnwell; 6,396 white men, 6,306 white women; 24 free colored blacks (18 men and 6 women); and 616 free mulattos (307 men and 309 women). The enslaved black slave population was 16,390 (7,970 men and 8,420 women). The enslaved mixed-race population numbered 1,011 (552 mulatto men and 459 mulatto women).[3]

Evidence from the witnesses' testimonies from the February 1858 trial and reported in the supreme court opinion expose Willis's transgressions of the boundaries of race and class "in a manner disreputable to the entire neighborhood, . . . and assailing the institution of slavery through a tolerated amalgamation."[4] Among those who testified were Willis's friends and acquaintances, including neighbors and others who saw him before he left for his voyage and during his travels. Jonathan Pender was a local overseer. He knew Willis from Williston, where they traded goods. He recalled that "Willis had no lawful wife or child; he was an industrious, money-making man."[5] On several occasions he visited Willis at home, where Pender noticed his living arrangements; in his house was "a negro woman named Amy, whom Wm. Kirkland had owned, and some three or four mulatto children."[6]

When Willis's friends and acquaintances visited, Amy remained unobtrusive and in the background. She did not present herself as his social equal. Nonetheless, it was common gossip that she was Willis's mistress and that the children were his: "there was a great deal in Willis's own behavior to confirm the belief."[7] Pender once had dinner at the house, observing Willis give the children the best food from the table; one of the smaller ones got onto his lap. As for Amy, her relationship to Willis indicated that she in some respects had gained a status far above than one would expect of a slave.

That Willis permitted Amy to reach a higher status than her race warranted was obvious to members of the white community. Amy acted as if she were free, white, and married to him. More than one individual had seen her riding in Willis's carriage in public. According to Pender, Amy was "trading largely, and as freely as a white woman, at Williston," including at the store owned by Willis's nephew James.[8] Reason Wooley and his wife Ary lived within a mile of Willis; he knew Willis about forty years. They appeared to be reasonably close: he "knew Amy, went to Willis' house often; worked a great deal for him; witness and Willis were usually very friendly." As far as Wooley understood the situation, "Willis knew that it was generally reported that he kept Amy and the children were his. Witness never heard him deny the report."[9] As a matter of fact, "Willis called the children his . . . acted as a father towards them, eat at his table, nurse them, &c."[10] Ary Wooley clarified: "Amy was the reputed concubine of Elijah Willis, or in other words, his housekeeper, who seemed to manage his housekeeping, and [they] acted pretty much as man and wife."[11] Indeed, according to William Beazley, owner of a store next to the train depot in Williston—from which Willis departed South Carolina—and the postowner for Barnwell County: she "often had plenty of money, and frequently bought without cash, on credit. The merchants generally let her have what she wanted, gave her a copy of the bill, and the next time the old man, Elijah Willis, would come to Williston, he would pay all such bills without objection or inquiry."[12]

But the nature of Willis's domestic arrangement meant that he could not protect his family in the traditional way; marriage to Amy was not an option under the law. As a result he had to leave South Carolina: "he traveled a great deal and spent a heap of money to fix [his] business."[13] Willis had gone to Cincinnati in 1854, where he retained the law firm of Jolliffe & Gitchell; James M. Gitchell drafted a will for him, and John Jolliffe agreed to serve as an executor. This will was the subject of an earlier action, *Jolliffe v. Fanning*, discussed in chapter 1. When Willis died in May 1855, John Jolliffe probated the Ohio will in Ohio. In the meantime, when those in South Carolina heard the news of his death but knowing nothing of the 1854 will, they probated the earlier 1846 will in which Willis left all his property to his white relatives. The litigation ensued when Jolliffe went to South Carolina in order to fulfill his responsibilities under the Ohio will. The South Carolina Supreme Court found the Ohio will to be valid in that first action. The white relatives then initiated the action in *Willis v. Jolliffe*, arguing that even if the will was valid, Amy and her family could not inherit because they were slaves.

Testifying in this second action, Woolley recalled that Willis had asked whether Wooley and his wife might be interested in joining him in relocating from South Carolina:

> He said he was doing well here, but he could not remain here and free his children, and let them have his property. He said he did not intend his people to have one cent of his property, if he could help it. He said, if he stayed here his relations would make slaves of Amy and her children; he said his relatives were gaping for his property, but they should not have it.[14]

Willis realized that greed and resentment of his familial situation fueled his relatives' response. He then planned measures to counteract them.

It is significant that by this time the legislature had barred manumission by deed and will. Willis therefore couldn't manumit in the state and draw up a will in favor of Amy and the children. If he had been married, it would have been irrelevant whether he wanted to make a will. If a man died intestate his widow could apply for letters of administration as his immediate heir. Thus estates probated in Barnwell in this period indicate that not all people made up wills. The ordinary, the administrator charged with probating estates, then set a court date for all creditors to bring forward their claims and for all claimants to the estate to assert their interests, including those who might object to the probating of the will, if there was one. The ordinary designated officials to inventory the estate: the property and the outstanding debts. The office had oversight over any sales of the assets that might be needed to cover the debts.

Challenges to the will were heard in the court of equity. All of the activity that went into the handling of estates presupposed legal capacity, and any white person with rights to an estate was thus empowered to challenge any bequests to slaves. There was no reason, then, for Willis's relatives to stand aside. Amy, as an enslaved woman, had no legal capacity, and thus no standing in the state of South Carolina. She could not claim status as his common-law wife. Thus Willis, in seeking to give bequests to Amy and the seven children, devised a careful manumission strategy combined with the judicious use of a will.

Making up a will in Ohio was thus a last-ditch strategy. He had the will drawn up the year before he died, and when he brought Amy and the others to Ohio, he was going to set them up there with money and property. He intended to return to South Carolina, sell everything, and rejoin them. Willis arrived in Cincinnati the day before the will was drafted. He introduced himself to Gitchell and Jolliffe and explained he wanted to make up a will and "provide for certain persons whom he held as slaves in South Carolina . . . he desired to make those slaves his heirs, and wished to find some persons of property and character in Ohio, who would consent to act as his executors."[15] Those to inherit were Amy and her seven children: Elder, Ellick, Phillip, Clarissa Ann, Julia Ann, Eliza Ann, and Savage. The lawyers found several individuals willing to serve as executors, including Edward Harwood and Andrew H. Ernst, but Willis insisted that Jolliffe be among the executors; Gitchell did not explain why.

After Willis finished the business of the will, he explained he would bring Amy and the others to Ohio in a year's time, but timing was important. Edward Harwood, one of those in Ohio who failed to qualify as executor, explained: "he was inclined to apoplexy, and was liable at any moment to be called away, for which reason he wished to make his will."[16] William Callum, another traveler on the train from Barnwell, recalled a conversation in which Willis said he hoped to settle the family on a farm somewhere out west and "school the children."[17] Gitchell never saw Willis alive again, testifying that he learned that Willis "had died upon the wharf, and I saw his corpse at the Dumas House, in this city, on the 21st day of May, 1855."[18]

Once Willis died and the will was probated, the other executors did not qualify as executors. Only Jolliffe did, which meant that as a member of the law partnership charged with drafting the will and as an executor charged with overseeing the resolution of the estate, he became an effective advocate when the will was challenged. Willis's shrewd strategy was significant not only for that reason, but also because he ensured that Amy and the others would be free. It meant that any challenges to the will based on his own state of mind would not succeed.

In the first action, those challenging the will alleged that Willis had made the will under Amy's influence, that he was under her control and unable to make a reasonable disposition of his property. There was no other reason, they argued, for him to have drawn up a will in her favor and contradicting the will he drafted several years before. Relying solely on some of the testimony as presented in the earlier case, one previous commentator did not offer a full study of Willis's character and behavior, describing him as "a chronic alcoholic whose visions of black avenging angels had apparently caused him to take them to free territory."[19]

Testifying in *Willis v. Jolliffe*, however, Andrew H. Ernst remembered about Willis that "his plans seemed to be well arranged. I think my interview fully justifies me in saying that he was then a man of sound and calculating mind."[20] He had been planning the move for a while, and Pender testified that Willis had once asked him if he knew anyone who might be interested in buying "his possessions in Barnwell—lands, negroes, stock, and everything else."[21] He spoke to

Beazley on another occasion: he was looking to find a buyer willing to pay \$35,000. But in 1850 and 1851, before he thought of selling, he talked to William Knotts about setting up a trust "of all his property, to be held by him, . . . for the support and benefit of two colored women, and the children of the younger of the two women; that he did not wish these women and the children ever to become slaves."[22] The older woman was Celia, referred to also as Ceilly or Cely. She was Amy's mother.

Knotts was a friend who had known him for about twenty-three years. He advised Willis not to use a trust: it would have been better to take the family to a free state. In an 1855 inventory of his estate done at his death, among the various entries that one would expect in the running of his farm and lumber business—namely domestic items, agricultural products and equipment, such as horses and mules—were listed at least thirty slaves. The assessors listed Amy and three of her children as his property, but they were in Cincinnati, Ohio, beyond the reach of those in South Carolina.[23]

Beazley recalled seeing them in May 1855 around the time they left Barnwell. Willis went to get his mail and bills; he owed the merchant some money. On the day he left he got to the train depot before Amy and the others: "they unloaded their baggage at the usual car landing, in front of witnesses' store."[24] Included in the party were "two black children of Amy, (the oldest of her children about grown when Elijah Willis left the State)."[25] According to the 1855 inventory the three children were: Elder, eighteen years old; Aleck, sixteen; and Phillip, about thirteen or fourteen. James Meredith, a conductor, remembered a conversation he had with Willis:

> In reply to a question, asked by me, E. Willis stated that he was not taking them to Hamburg for sale, but was on his way to Cincinnati, Ohio, with them, and my recollection is that he spoke of them as his family. He had, as baggage, several new trunks, and no such luggage as negroes usually carry. The negroes were all dressed in much better style than is usual with negroes; and Mr. Willis sat with them in the car nearly all the time.[26]

There is no record of Amy's feelings or thoughts about the trial, or of the nature of her relationship with Willis, who was of a different race, twenty years her senior, and born and raised in an entirely different social sphere. As a slave Amy had no right to testify at all under South Carolina law, even though she was a beneficiary of the will at issue in the court.

Although Willis's domestic arrangements were widely known in the neighborhood, not everyone approved. Dr. John G. Guignard recalled an evening when Willis visited him: "We were not encumbered by company, and as it were *tete-a-tete*, he conversed freely, stating that his situation was apparent to his neighbors, distressing to him. That the connection he formed was evidently unpleasant to his relations and disreputable."[27] On another occasion Guignard was at Willis's house: "in presence of F. W. Matthews, suggest[ed] to him in strong terms the propriety of shaking off his connection with Amy, and endeavoring to regain his proper position in society."[28]

Some whites would have seen him as living not as a man of his class and race but as though he was black and on equal social footing with slaves—which is to say no social status at all. Pender remembered that when news reached South Carolina of Willis's death, he spoke to James and Michael Willis, two members of Elijah's extended family. James reported that his uncle had been buried in a Cincinnati graveyard reserved for negroes; Pender "asked why they did not fetch his body home," to which Willis retorted that "he carried himself there, and he may lie there."[29] His relatives, friends, and acquaintances dealt with him as a white man because he was one of them: a planter and businessman of some wealth in the community, and in the founding family.[30]

Some of those signing the 1860 petition were men who had known Willis, including Johnson Hagood, the commissioner in Equity, who in 1852 signed a certificate of character presented into evidence at the trial, in which was stated "we are well acquainted with Mr. Elijah Willis. . . . [H]e is a gentleman of unimpeached character and standing."[31] Willis was considering taking Amy and the others to Maryland where they might be set up "at trades in that State, and has desired of us this certificate, which we cheerfully give."[32] It is understandable why the firm of Jolliffe & Gitchell would want that document put into evidence; it indicated that notwithstanding the allegations of those who claimed Willis was not of sound mind and of worthless character, outstanding men in the community were once willing to vouch for his character and integrity.

But the men of Barnwell understood their right to petition their government. These were men who felt they had some stake in their community, its direction, and the morals of the young men in the community who might have followed Willis's example. Most interesting of all was A. P. Bogacki. In 1850 he was a thirty-year-old, unmarried Polish immigrant and merchant worth $1,300. He knew Willis; in 1854 he witnessed to a sale of land that Willis made to A. T. Hutto, and by 1860, he had married into the Willis family.[33] But he was then worth only $500. His wife Eliza was one of Willis's nieces but was not listed as inheriting under the 1846 will, in which only Willis's siblings and their spouses appeared to be legatees. In the 1860 census Bogacki was described as a forty-eight-year-old salesman; he and Eliza had three children, all under the age of eight.[34]

At the probating of the 1846 South Carolina will, Bogacki was among the thirty individuals listed as "distributees of Elijah Willis," members of his extended family who would inherit the estate if the Ohio will were found invalid.[35] Included also were James and Michael Willis, already mentioned. Bogacki and the two Willises thus had a direct interest in the litigation, and white men living openly with black and mulatto women could result, as it threatened to do in the Willis case, in white relatives and in-laws being denied access to the inheritance. Younger white men without much property, such as Bogacki, saw their future inheritance at stake.

The state legislature referred the petition to the House of Representatives Committee on Colored Population, chaired by J. Harleston Read. The committee reported on November 29, 1860, their determination that "the evil complained of cannot be prevented by legislation," and that it therefore could not "recommend additional legislation thereon."[36] Unable or unwilling to regulate the private domestic arrangements of white men, the petition was tabled on December 17, 1860.[37]

As we've already seen, the 1820 requirement that owners seeking to free slaves petition the legislature was an attempt to curtail the growth of a free black population by denying owners agency and by funneling all manumission requests through a state body. All freed blacks were to emigrate, pursuant to law, or be fined and forced back into servitude. They could not return to the state.[38]

The change in procedure caught many unaware. Not only did men who sought to free their enslaved partners and children find themselves caught in a bind, but so did owners seeking to fulfill promises to retire older slaves, and free blacks seeking to emancipate enslaved relatives. They believed they would always be able to manumit through the process set forth by the state legislature in 1800, which required only that an owner appear with an enslaved person before a local magistrate and submit to questioning by five local freeholders from the community about "the character of the said slave or slaves, and his, her or their ability to gain a livelihood in an honest way."[39] On successful inquiry the examiners certified that the owner could free the slave by written deed.[40] As a result of the 1820 procedure, petitions poured in from all over the state, including Barnwell.

But this use of the petition in slavery issues was different from that making general claims for money owed by the government or as a means of citizens claiming entitlements, such as pensions.[41] Instead, the petition process was more akin to the first-amendment right to petition government for grievances. Those petitioners discussed in this section complained about the unfairness of the new statutory provisions limiting their abilities to manumit their slaves privately, but they nonetheless followed the new rule. After the 1820 legislation testamentary manumission became more difficult because of the new procedures: owners using that method now had to rely on their executors or others to carry their petitions before the legislature, rather than have the matter settled locally. As we see below, significant among the arguments raised by the post-1820 petitioners was that some provisions had been made on the behalf of those slaves to be manumitted: children inheriting the property that would enable their independence and support. Such slaves would thus not degenerate upon becoming free—financial independence meant they need not resort to criminal activity in order to support themselves.

Among the petitioners was Henry Ravenel of Berkeley district in St. Johns, executor of his uncle, Paul, who died in 1820. Henry was charged "in special confidence" to emancipate a family of slaves: Else and her five children named Beck, Harry, John, James, and Nancy, and Beck's child William. Claiming that all of them had been well provided for by the estate, he argued that the new rule operated as an ex post facto law and was thus unconstitutional; it had "an operation decidedly retrospective," denying freedom to those who had "been long in fact tho not in form, discharged from service."[42] Others treated them like free people, but they had no official documents of emancipation. Ravenel hoped they would be freed and permitted to remain in the state.

George Bellinger of Colleton district complained that as a result of legislation he was "completely frustrated" in his attempt to free three of his infant slaves."[43] He explained that he was fully aware that the operation of the law of wills would permit him to free the slaves; moreover, he had already written a will "with the advice said of counsel learned in the law." But that was not enough for him, as he emphatically stated in his petition: "your petitioner, like every other individual of mankind, perhaps without a single exception, wishes to complete by his own immediate agency an act, so highly interesting and agreeable to himself, rather than have it be done by others after his death."[44]

Bellinger didn't explain why this was so important to him, but he was aware of the uses of law in this context. He drafted a will but wanted to do more. Perhaps the children he cared so much about were his biological children whose welfare was at the forefront of his mind. He wanted to secure their futures immediately, while they were still young, and not wait. Perhaps he was aware that his desires could be thwarted if he were to rely upon the use of a will to effectuate the children's manumission. He couldn't imagine the legislature included children among those of "depraved character" and incapable of taking care of themselves, like those such who had been emancipated by imprudent owners in the past. Those were the slaves the legislature hoped to keep in bondage. Beyond that, children were not emancipated and thrown out of society to fend for themselves. Instead, he suggested in the case of the children under his care, "their maintenance and their being brought up in an industrious manner, could be sufficiently served by their emancipation." The legislature agreed with his arguments and manumitted because he had offered "bond and surety," but it was not generous in manumitting others.[45]

In 1827 David Martin of Barnwell petitioned to emancipate his two enslaved daughters, Eliza born in 1812 and Martha born in 1817, so that they might enjoy his property. The legislative committee recommended, with no explanation, "that the prayer not be granted."[46] Undeterred, Martin in his will directed his executors to free the children and their mother Lucy. They were to liquidate his assets and give them his entire estate. In the interim, however, he took the children and their mother to Kentucky and freed them there. He then returned to South Carolina, where he was described in the 1830 census as a man in his forties and living alone.[47] Thus, after his death in 1831, Lucy was able to withstand the challenges of Martin's mother, siblings, and an estranged wife who claimed to have rights to the estate, even though the last had filed for separation in 1815. The court ruled Lucy and the children were entitled to the bulk of it.[48]

William Dunn, also of Barnwell, sought to emancipate a twelve-year-old slave named William ten years later. The child's mother was described as "light yellow" and his father as white, but the older William did not name the father, noting only that he owned the child. In the words of Dunn, the boy was "nevertheless so very white and of so good a complexion" that he could pass for white. He would not "create even a suspicion on the mind of the most critical observer" that he was of black heritage. Beyond that, he was not raised among blacks; as a result, he had "not imbibed any of the principles or habits peculiar to them."[49] Although Dunn hoped William would be manumitted and permitted to remain in the state, the petition died in committee.

In denying a petition filed by William B. Farr of Union in 1823, the legislature ignored the petitioner's evidence that the people to be freed would not become public charges. Although the legislators could sympathize with the appeals, the interests of the greater white community and their perception of freed blacks were more important: "their [the slaves'] situation is really worste [sic] and more to be deplored than those slaves who enjoy the protection of good owners."[50] In their view freed blacks became criminals; they fell into idleness and exercised poor judgment. It was "against the policy and safety of the country to have any slaves emancipated."[51] Thus the committee also rejected the petition of Jeremiah Dickey, a free man of color who claimed that prior to marrying him his wife had a child by her owner, Robert Manning of York District. He purchased the child, Jinsey, raised her as his, and had hoped to emancipate her under the name "Jinsey Dickey."

In our consideration of the Barnwell manumission petitions filed over the thirty years between David Martin's 1827 petition and the 1860 petition filed by the young men of Barnwell, it is useful to know something about those who sponsored the petitions and submitted them to the legislature.[52] The Angus Patterson who signed the 1860 petition was living in a different time than his father, also named Angus, who was born in the late 1700s. The eldest Patterson was the state senator for the Barnwell district from 1822 to 1849 who sponsored the 1827 petition on behalf of David Martin. A lawyer, he represented Lucy Martin in her effort to defend her right to David Martin's property. He also signed off on the certificate of good character and standing that Elijah Willis needed in order to go to Maryland and free Amy and her children (though Willis ultimately took them to Ohio). John Bauskett was among his cohort; he signed neither the certificate of good standing nor the petition. As representative for the Edgefield legislative district from 1834 to 1838, he filed instead William Dunn's 1837 petition to manumit. But most importantly, he served as cocounsel to the Ohio lawyers in defending the will of Elijah Willis in the contest. He also represented Lucy Martin in claiming rights to David Martin's estate.

On the other hand, the younger Patterson lived in a community in which men like him were worried about the transfer of property from whites to blacks, and he stood with them in support of curtailing inheritance rights by blacks. Signatory John M. Whetstone was a lawyer and legislator for Barnwell who submitted the 1860 petition in the House of Representatives. He was not part of the cohort that included the elder Patterson and Bauskett. One might wonder what caused the men of Barnwell to demonstrate in 1860 such contrary and divergent views from those shown by their older cohort after the 1820 petition requirement? In the first group, attorneys Bauskett

Justice John B. O'Neall,
ca. 1840. Courtesy of
South Caroliniana Library,
University of South Carolina,
Columbia.

and the elder Patterson were slaveholders; in the second group, lawyers Hutson and Whetstone were both born after 1820. Whatever
public pressure might have fallen on lawyers in the years immediately
preceding the Civil War, Bauskett was far more active than those later
lawyers in protecting manumission rights, insofar as he was a prac-
ticing lawyer defending rights to manumit—much like Justice John
Belton O'Neall as a lawyer in private practice and later on the state
supreme court.

The presence of these lawyers at different times on the bench,
in the legislature, and in their private practices indicates a fluidity
of lawyer's professionalism in the early and mid-nineteenth century
that is worth noting. Prior to the institutionalization of the legal profession in the late nineteenth century, those interested in becoming lawyers studied with seasoned practitioners and read treatises on
the principles of law. That is how O'Neall learned the profession,
studying law with John Caldwell and borrowing books from Judge
Anderson Crenshaw of Alabama.[53] But there is no indication in his
discussion of his life, of what led to his more liberal position on slav-

ery and the law; his practice appeared to have been the motivating factor. He was fully aware of the paradoxes of slavery and of the failures of the law to address them.

On the state supreme court Chief Justice John Belton O'Neall and the other judges, Job Johnstone and F. H. Wardlaw, confronted a serious legal issue in the Willis case: were Amy and the others free and capable of taking their bequest under the will, or were they slaves pursuant to the law of South Carolina? O'Neall, in writing for the court, reasoned that under the Northwest Ordinance and Ohio's constitution, none of the nine could be slaves. Ohio was their new domicile, not South Carolina, the domicile of Willis. He no longer owned them; he had told everyone before he left that he was going to Ohio for a short period of time, to return after settling Amy and the others there.

Even though South Carolina set forth stringent requirements for manumission, it was within the right of Ohio to confer freedom on those slaves who reached its borders, as a matter of internal policy. Willis made sure his family all reached Ohio; they became free as a result, according to Chief Justice O'Neall:

> They are in the enjoyment of freedom, and we cannot and ought not interfere. . . . I should feel myself degraded if . . . I trampled on law and constitution, in obedience to popular will. There is no law in South Carolina which, notwithstanding the freedom of Amy and her children, declares the trusts in their favor are void. . . . they are capable of becoming the [beneficiaries] under his will."[54]

O'Neall disagreed strongly with the 1858 trial court opinion in *Willis v. Jolliffe*, written by Justice David L. Wardlaw, who held that they did not become free because Willis did not accomplish the manumission before he died. Their domicile as slaves followed that of their owner, and because Willis had not moved to Ohio by the time of his death, Amy and the others were still resident in South Carolina, and it was that state's laws of property that governed them and determined his ability to free them. But O'Neall's view won the day in 1860.

O'Neall had long prior to this opinion developed his views on slavery and the law, and they comported with his decision in the Willis case. Rejecting both the act of 1820 "declaring that no slave should hereafter be emancipated, but by Act of the Legislature" and the Act of 1841, which made void any attempt by will to have slaves removed from the state and freed, O'Neall restated from a treatise of twelve years earlier: "my experience as a man, and a Judge, lead me to condemn [these laws]. They ought to be repealed, and the Act of 1800 restored. The State has nothing to fear from emancipation, regulated as that law directs it to be. Many an owner knows that he has a slave or slaves, for whom he feels it to be his duty to provide. As the law now stands, that cannot be done."[55] The Act of 1800 had sought to control manumissions of those slaves "of bad or depraved character, or, from age or infirmity, incapable of gaining their livelihood by honest means."[56] Manumission could take place by deed; the owner could appear before a local magistrate and fulfill the procedures to emancipate: answer all questions touching on the slave's character and ability for self-support. In Justice O'Neall's view, case law later extended this rule to bequests for freedom granted in wills.

Most importantly, however, the prerogatives of owners should not be curtailed: "All laws unnecessarily restraining the rights of owners are unwise. So far as may be necessary to preserve the peace and good order of the community, they may be properly restrained."[57] His perception of why the act of 1841 was passed presaged what happened in the Willis case a decade later: "This act, it has always been said, was passed to control a rich gentleman in the disposition of his estate. Like everything of the kind, he defeated it, and the expectations of his next of kin, by devising his estate to one of his kindred, to the exclusion of all the rest."[58] Willis's behavior and his reasons for visiting Ohio to draft a will and thereafter relocate indicate that Amy and her children were his kindred, so to speak; however, his white next of kin — the host of siblings, in-laws, nieces, and nephews — were not those to whom he was closest. His behavior suggested he understood that these legal heirs would seize the entirety of his estate and enslave his family. Knowing that the law of South Carolina would permit this, he made alternative legal arrangements and pursued a strategy to ensure his wishes would be fulfilled.

O'Neall did not fully explain what led him to a liberal position on manumission and to support Willis's tactics to manumit. But O'Neall was fully aware that slave owners often had enslaved partners and children who they wished to manumit and give property. Moreover, he knew the objections that white men in those communities had to such dispositions. In at least one case he agreed to serve as an executor for a slave owner seeking to give his estate to favored slaves: an enslaved partner and their son.[59] William Farr, from Union, submitted in 1822 and 1823 petitions to the legislature to "free Fanny, a mulatto woman" in her early twenties, and the son she had by him, six-year-old Henry. State Senator James McKibben from the Union legislative district sponsored Farr's petition, which explained that she was "upright, honest, and perfectly capable of her own support." In 1823 John F. Fewell, also of Union, vouched for her and that he knew her to be the property of Farr; she was honest, truthful, and faithful. When the petitions were denied, O'Neall made up a will for Farr in 1828 and agreed to serve as legatee and executor on behalf of Fanny and Henry, according to written instructions declaring the trust arrangement. In another case O'Neall was coexecutor of the last will and testament of John Kelly Sr. of Newberry. He and the other executor submitted a petition to the legislature to free "a negro fellow named Nathaniel" in accordance with the terms of the will. There was no indication of the reasons why the owner wanted him freed. The petition was denied by the judiciary committee.[60]

O'Neall was of the same age group and cohort as Bauskett—the local attorney in the Willis case—and the elder Angus Patterson. From 1816 to 1828 he was in private law practice and served as a member of the House of Representatives for the Newberry district before his election to the judiciary in 1828. He joined the court of appeals in 1830.[61] Perhaps he was willing to hold for testators on the bench because the legislature seized control over the manumission process, at the prodding of local white men, in order to curtail owners' prerogatives, something with which he disagreed.[62] It seems that O'Neall was deferential to wishes of late owners because as white men they had the right to own property and relinquish, if they so chose.

But the legislature, prodded by discontented whites who petitioned their legislature, sought to undermine the type of trust arrangements he had set up while in practice. For example, on November 12, 1840, two groups of white men from the Union District, next door to O'Neall's community of Newberry, filed a petition in order to receive clarification of the law on slaves' property rights. They were responding to language in *Farr*, an opinion written by Justice Baylis J. Earle for the entire court:

> We cannot, however, avoid seeing, through the face of the will, that the purpose was to provide a mode of bestowing the property on the issue of an illicit intercourse between that slave and himself. We do not choose here to speak of the indecency of such a connection, nor of the policy of permitting property to be given or devised in trust for the benefit of such persons. Until the Legislature thinks fit to interfere, we must have questions of this sort determined by the established rules of law.[63]

The men of Union rose to the court's challenge and placed their petition before the legislature. According to the signers of the petition, they were of the perception that it was:

> [R]ecognized by the courts of South Carolina as a Legal principle that a slave cannot own property of any kind — But that a man having the right to give his property to whomever he pleases under some slight statutory restrictions. May will his property to any free white man, in Trust or in secret trust for or to the Beneficial use of a Slave. And this even to the disinherison [*sic*] of his own offspring or other heirs at Law.[64]

In their view any such policy would be "an indecent trust," and "repugnant alike to sound policy, the genius of our institutions."[65] Barring slaves from owning property was proper and necessary, but they noted "that principle clearly violated by permitting that to be no effect done indirectly by the intervention of a trustee which by the positive Law of the Land is forbid to be done directly."[66]

Not only did trusts permit slaves to own property, but such arrangements gave them a measure of independence from their owners and gave them avenues to manumission through access to monetary resources. The men of Union wrote plainly about the inevitable result: "Give the slave money . . . and you place it in his power at once to place himself beyond the reach of servitude — Money is Power, and none need live in servitude who can command it."[67] They imagined that if an owner could convey property in a trust for his own slave, the following could happen: slave owner B wills property to C for the benefit of A's slave as part of a secret trust, in which any one of the petitioners could be A, ignorant that he was at risk for losing a valuable slave. B, in their minds, should have no such right, and the first line of defense was curtailing the trust altogether.

The trust arrangement could become the means of slaves to use their agency to escape the vicissitudes of slavery. Not only might a slave be able to find sympathetic whites nearby willing to help, but considering the petitioners' logic, the trust could become a tool for abolitionists who might identify slaves seeking freedom, or who might coordinate with owners seeking to free their slaves. In the miscegenation context it could become the tool of enslaved women seeking freedom. An alliance with a powerful man who was not her owner could result in her securing property she might need to buy her freedom or to escape to a free state.

Not only could trust arrangements result in the loss of enslaved property but it would "in effect, extend the Law as to trusts for us to embrace our entire slave population into its provisions—and thus in effect hold out encouragement to amalgamation and in all but the name recognize the Equality of the slave with the Freeman in an important Branch of our civil jurisprudence."[68]

The petitioners might well have thought that once slaves had equal rights under the law they would meet whites on levels of social equality, leading to "amalgamation," a mixing of the races. But that mixing of the races was already occurring, resulting in the creating of families and the use of trusts and estates law for the upkeep of partners and children barred from manumission and inheritance rights under the law of slavery. Nonetheless, the legislature reacted to the petition as the men of Union hoped they would: with the act of 1841, which barred manumission by deed and proclaimed void any trusts that would permit slaves to be manumitted or that would grant them nominal slave status.[69]

Perhaps both the 1840 and 1860 petitions were direct jabs at O'Neall, whose election to the state legislature "gave him the opportunity of being more generally known."[70] Thus the men might have been aware of O'Neall's involvement in *Farr*—not least because

William Farr resided in Union. There were 167 signatories to that petition, and 50 to the 1860 petition. But note that notwithstanding the act of 1841, Justice O'Neall, writing for the court in *Carmille v. Adm'r of Carmille et al.* two years later, held that the "Act has been supposed to be retrospective, but on carefully considering it, I think all its provisions are future, and I rejoice that they are so. For I should have thought it a stain upon the purity of our legislation, if it had been true that the Act had been passed to defeat vested rights."[71]

Thus O'Neall rejected the hysteria over manumission in the legislature that threatened private rights. He envisioned that the social order of slavery could be a benevolent one, predicated on mutual obligations stemming from paternalism. It was, as he wrote, in owners' interests to ensure such a slave society, and the law's role was to inaugurate it:

> Experience and observation fully satisfy me that the first law of slavery is that of kindness from the owner to the slave. With that properly inculcated, enforced by law and judiciously applied, slavery becomes a family relation, next to its attachments to that of a parent and child. . . . With such feelings on our plantations, what have we to fear from fanaticism? Our slaves would be our sentinels to watch over us, our defenders to protect our firesides from those prowling harpies, who preach freedom and steal slaves from their happy homes.[72]

We have already examined O'Neall's language and position as being that of a paternalist supporter of slavery, not that of an abolitionist, though that doesn't explain how he appears today to have been so liberal. A. E. Keir Nash asserts that, in general, analysis of "judges' socio-economic characteristics simply does not help much" in explaining a judge such as O'Neall.[73] But in O'Neall's case, background may have had a significant influence upon his judicial views. Born in Newberry, O'Neall was not a member of the old slaveholding elite families of South Carolina. He came from an Irish-American Quaker family, and his father owned a store. In 1810 his father experienced a mental breakdown and, as O'Neall wrote later, was "deprived of his reason, . . . Bankruptcy came down upon him, and his creditors nearly crushed every hope by suing him in his unfortunate insane condition, and forcing his property to sale at an immense sacrifice. Thus his family were turned out of doors."[74] O'Neall was someone who had direct experience in how the law could oppress as well as empower.

Considering earlier historical analyses of Jacksonian politics, O'Neall's presentation of his own life story makes him sound like a Jacksonian self-made man. His family appeared to be well-to-do but not wealthy, particularly after his father's bankruptcy. Thus O'Neall's school expenses were paid in part by himself, and the rest out of his "father[']s dilapidated estate."[75] Beyond that, he was a member of the temperance movement; he also rejected the use of tobacco. He might very well have been a reformer, and as Nash suggests, his treatise on South Carolina slave law "was a policy document recommending far-going liberalization of the South Carolina Slave Code."[76]

Contemporary commentators provide a sense of how O'Neall was seen at the time, and one commentator who did a retrospective on him verged on hagiography: "But it is a more grateful task to speak of him when he was transferred from the Bar to the Bench; to present him as a Judge, as a minister of Justice—as the crowned head of his profession, so to speak—presiding in our highest courts of Judicature with a dignity and honor worthy of his exalted position."[77] Little attention was paid to O'Neall's views on slavery, however. Celebrated as an educator, a judge, and as a temperance advocate, his ideas on slavery did not appear to be the focus of discussion during his lifetime or upon his death.[78]

The local men raised legal cases and issues of concern to them in their petition, but without addressing the roles of judges like O'Neall who decided those cases in ways with which they disagreed. They explained the social practices that troubled them and explained that in their view the legislators—the ones charged with determining the organic law that guided those very judges in their determinations—should establish different guidelines and rules.

On the other hand it is possible that notions of honor pervaded the nature of the responses and colored the petition to outlaw miscegenation. Historian Edward Ayers once explained that the social standing of southern men was predicated on how one was perceived: in the eyes of public opinion, men wondered whether they were treated with the respect due to a man of their stature. Men did not challenge honor on a whim, and "[h]onor, the overweening concern with the opinions of others, led people to pay particular attention to manners, to ritualized evidence of respect."[79] Thus those who objected to Willis's behavior appeared to contradict themselves. On the one hand, some contemporaries who had known him for a very long time called him an honorable man who dealt well and fairly with others, and they therefore might not have felt free to challenge him openly. They might instead have just talked behind his back, and might have minimized their social interactions with him.

Nonetheless, Willis's relatives might have felt compelled to bring the lawsuit to challenge the will, not only to recover assets that were to go to slaves but to recapture their familial honor. According to unwritten but fixed southern male codes of miscegenation, sex across the color line was tolerated as long as it took place in secret, the woman and her children were not officially recognized, and as long as they were not introduced to white society. By living openly with an enslaved woman as his partner, Willis subverted community mores and tarnished the family name. When his relatives challenged the will they reasserted their place as the legitimate members of his family. Although doing so meant being vocal about their displeasure, the "airing of dirty laundry" might have served to vindicate them and remove from them Willis's taint. Once the courts could no longer prevent the transfer of property, they hoped the legislature would solve the problem by authorizing local sheriffs to do the work for them, but at that point the legislature refused to become involved.

Subsequent to the South Carolina Supreme Court decision, on February 7, 1861, appraisers appointed by the probate court assessed the personal property owned by the Willis estate. It was all worth about $23,500, of which approximately $19,900 was in thirty-four slaves.[80] John Jolliffe, as Amy's attorney, was unable to manage the estate from Ohio, but he gave John Bauskett, the Columbia attorney who worked on both Willis cases, authorization to act on his behalf, in receiving money and property owned by the estate. Hugh E. Phillips, one of Willis's brothers-in-law, was the manager of the properties.[81]

It is unclear whether Amy and the other beneficiaries of Willis's second will received profits from the estate once the court held they were entitled to inherit, but it is significant that two years later, during the height of the Civil War, the estate was seized by the Confederate States of America, District of South Carolina, in an action brought by John J. Ryan, receiver of sequestered estates, against Bauskett and Phillips, as the estate's representatives. Willis had been dead for almost a decade, but Amy and the others, as inheritors, were found not to be loyal southerners. Their property in South Carolina, including 3,600 acres of land, was thus subject to seizure.[82] They might have gotten some land back, however. After the war ended Amy filed a lawsuit in probate court to demand an accounting and administration of the remainder of the estate.[83] As a result, between 1870 and 1873 Bauskett sold several pieces of land; Amy and the children were the vendors, living in Ohio.[84]

Although the census taker there might have listed her as Mary Ash, the census records otherwise seem to correspond with her history: a black woman born in South Carolina, the parent of several children born there, sharing the names of the children described in the official court records and conveyance books. The ages of all of them appeared to coincide with the ages they would have had in the 1850s. By this time Amy was a forty-seven-year-old housewife, married to Manuel Ash, a fifty-nine-year-old mulatto from North Carolina. He worked in a brickyard, as did the younger Elijah, fifteen years old. Julia was a domestic servant, twenty years old. Her other children were in school: Ann, thirteen, and John, twelve. Amy and her children had new lives in Athens, Ohio.

The Elijah Willis story ended with Amy Ash née Willis, the former enslaved partner of a slaveholding man, living in Ohio and suing in probate court in the state where she was once a slave. This phenomenon indicates the significance of the use of law in the context of cases such as these, and the overriding importance of geography linked to the use of legal institutions. Amy could only sue in South Carolina by operation of geography. Willis removed her from the clutches of a system in which she was considered property, in a carefully crafted strategy that employed mobility. By taking her by train and steamboat to Ohio from South Carolina, he took advantage of the diverging legal cultures that had developed on the eve of the Civil War. His extralegal measure ensured the legal measures he pursued.

Ohio, courtesy of the Northwest Ordinance, did not permit slavery within its borders. As a result, it became a receiving state for runaway slaves, slaveholders sending their slaves to escape slavery, or slave-owning partners and fathers of slaves seeking to manumit when their state laws did not permit emancipation within their borders. But in the case of Willis the dual strategy of using both geography and a last will and testament indicated even more so the significance of the operation of the law enabling Amy to be transformed from property to property owner. Because Willis had a new will drawn up in Ohio, the prior South Carolina will had no effect. Thus under that will she was listed in the inventory of the estate but was unaccounted for. She had become a free woman of color.

But becoming free did not necessarily mean she could ensure her property rights in South Carolina. Because the law of property in her home state was so infused with the ideology of slavery, she could not return to the state and enforce her inheritance rights. She had to rely on proxies—lawyers and relatives of her deceased partner—to protect her interests. That some were the same people who had objected to her inheritance meant that she had no guarantee they would protect and enforce her rights. Thus, long after the Civil War ended, she filed suit to gain access to the property.

The situation was not without its ironies, however. Willis was a slave owner who did not appear to have any internal conflicts over owning slaves and making his livelihood from their labor, or over singling out one of those slaves for his munificence, treating her as though she were free. But in the greatest of ironies Amy inherited property wrought from the labor of other enslaved blacks, over whom she had measures of privilege as the enslaved partner of a white man determined to give her all his property. That was exactly what the signers of the petition realized and were most fearful of: the possibility of former slaves inheriting estates that put them on equal footing to those within the cohort of the owner class. Thus, they filed their petition, hoping to root out the evil of white male–black female miscegenation in their midst.

That the measure failed indicates the level of privilege men like Willis enjoyed. As an elite white man he could live with an enslaved woman as his partner with no fear of real censure in the form of legal remedies that might be taken against him. Gossip and social ostracism could be ignored or avoided, as he planned to do by relocating to Ohio. He could just sell off his property and move to a state where he could live as freely as he liked. Even though South Carolina law told him he had no right to liberate his enslaved partner and family and give them his property, no one had the right to tell him he couldn't circumvent that law. He was thus empowered by the law in his ability to travel and conduct his business, whether buying, selling, or distributing property. This was the ultimate hallmark of being an elite white man in the antebellum South.

We believe that sexual politics under patriarchy is as pervasive in black women's lives as are the politics of class and race. We also find it difficult to separate race from class from sex oppression because in our lives they are most often experienced simultaneously.

— COMBAHEE RIVER COLLECTIVE, "A Black Feminist Statement"

CONCLUSION

The Law's Paradox of Property and Power

The Significance of Geography

THIS BOOK IS UNIQUE insofar as it demonstrates the significance of what Ariela Gross has described as a cultural approach to legal history, an investigation into "trial records in order to view the law from other perspectives—not only that of the judge but those of witnesses, litigants, jurors, and even slaves."[1] It explores the "confrontation between ordinary people and the apparatus of the state, and thus provid[ing] an opportunity for historians to explore power relations at a level closer to people's actual lives."[2]

Fathers of Conscience demonstrates the process by which judges of the state high courts of the antebellum South negotiated the interests of white wealth and white supremacy through will contests in which white men left bequests of freedom and property to enslaved and free black women and to the mixed-race children they bore the men. Put simply, the will contest, more than the mere transfer of property upon death, illuminates the most significant aspect of this book: the clash of values. It was a conflict among elites, and at stake was whether a white man could exercise the prerogatives of his race and class. He certainly could exercise his prerogative to have sex with black women, notwithstanding societal taboos against interracial sex. As a single or widowed man he was not constrained by conventional marriage to a white woman.

But he was not necessarily able to exercise his prerogative as a white man to do with his property as he saw fit. He could not always fulfill what he saw were his moral obligations, namely to give the women and his mixed-race children their freedom and his property. The testator's relatives, entitled by their own prerogatives of legitimacy and whiteness, could sue to secure his property for themselves: the women and children at the heart of the will contest, and the money and real property he hoped to give them. Attacking a man as degraded or vulnerable, they explained why his will should not stand: he was incompetent or enthralled by a black woman who was permitted improper intimacies. The challengers were successful or not depending on the specific laws in their jurisdiction and on whether the high court judges who heard their cases agreed.

Geography was important, not only because the cases examined here arose in different states that developed different approaches to manumission. From a state like Kentucky that had liberal manumission laws in place to states like South Carolina and Mississippi, whose legislatures made manumission more difficult over time, geography played a role. When manumission became difficult, geography affected which strategy testators pursued to convey their property as they wished. A last will and testament bequeathing freedom and property could be reinforced by effecting the manumission elsewhere. This strategy greatly improved the beneficiaries' ability to inherit; they could then use their status as free people of color with rights to sue for property, an avenue not available to them as slaves.

But their ability to sue as free people of color, or even to establish a right to freedom, was dependent on the decision of judges on the courts of appeal. Sympathetic judges respected testators' paternal instincts, while those who were unsympathetic obeyed the formal laws of slavery, reinforcing the white social order, retaining white wealth, and protecting the white heirs from having to recognize their enslaved relatives. Judges taking the latter view gave the white relatives what they wanted: the money and property that black people would otherwise have received. On the other hand, beneficiaries who were successful became members of the black elite, people of freedom and property.

This book thus provides an important link for demonstrating the development of a pre–Civil War black and mixed-race elite. It originated in people who got their freedom long before most blacks did, and among them were enslaved black women and their mixed-race black children freed within their home states of the South, or brought to the North and there freed. They were then able to live as free people with some money and property. Notwithstanding difficulties they experienced as free people of color without the same rights as whites, they were victorious. They escaped slavery to present themselves in written records as free people with rights. The key link in these instances was a white male progenitor who freed them during his lifetime or who gave them bequests of freedom after his death.

But there is no hagiography here in describing these men as benevolent patriarchs. Each act of heroism was infused with the villainy of slavery. Slave owners who fathered biological children by women they owned did so in a rigid system in which the inequality of status between them and the women raises the question of whether those relationships were consensual, particularly when the women were nameless and faceless but their children were identified as beneficiaries. Nonetheless, sympathetic judges hearing their cases could see the men as heroic in that their behavior in the end mitigated their past transgressions.

The beneficiaries named to receive bequests pursuant to the will of a deceased white man reinforced their own class privileges over other enslaved blacks. Their heroism in pursuing their rights was also tainted by slavery. They did not create the system of slavery, its corresponding laws or conventions, but they hoped to gain from it. Their progenitors gave them the ability to pursue these goals. The wealth these beneficiaries sought was built through their own slave labor and that of others, and in absolute identification with the owner class they wanted to access the property that would give them financial independence. Where funds were insufficient to pay their legacies, slaves could be sold in order that they become enriched.

As for the judicial patriarchs, perhaps the sympathetic judges were heroic insofar as they respected the testators' bequests in the face of community pressure to reject them. When the common law or statutory law favored the wills, they upheld. But these were not saintly abolitionists and freedom fighters: often they were slave owners and, as judges for states that sanctioned slavery, they were part of the slave regime. Nonetheless, some, like O'Neall, could put aside political demands against manumission and fears of a financially empowered free black population because they adhered to a view of the rule of law that made them reluctant to permit passions and prejudices to influence judicial determinations. Testators' wishes were far more important in their view. Even when they were troubled by testators who crossed racial boundaries and knew that the community also objected, they could put aside those political concerns and focus on what was important: respect for the individual men's property rights.

As men occupying a conservative role in society, such judges believed their role was solely to protect property rights; the right to hold property also entailed the right to relinquish property. If that right to relinquish meant a slave became freed and inherited property, that was, after all, the hallmark of individual rights in Anglo-American jurisprudence. The testators wished to relinquish their property and perhaps atone for their past indiscretions. The law should not be used to deny them their last wishes. To do so would destroy property rights and imperil everyone's right of ownership.

This study of appellate cases from courts of the antebellum South explains the importance of legal institutions in identifying an anomalous population: white male partners of enslaved women who fathered their mixed-race enslaved children. As men living beyond the pale, they could be written off by their white families, as in the case of Willis, or the fact of their mixed-race enslaved children ignored or forgotten. But their legacies lived on. Scholars of African American history have long been aware of oral histories demonstrating the existence of such a population, and it has not been a secret that many members of the nineteenth-century black bourgeoisie had their roots in miscegenation: mixed-race men and women who had access to privilege and whose white benefactors manumitted them, provided funds for their upkeep, and made it possible for them to learn trades.

Fathers of Conscience thus explains trusts and estates law as a unique avenue for black empowerment in the nineteenth century. Slavery was about property rights. Owners had the right to own slaves and profit from their labor. On the other hand, trusts and estates law determined who would receive property upon an owner's death. Trusts and estates law could thus be used to circumvent the law of slavery that would have denied manumission and access to wealth. But this also means that manumissions under circumstances that did not require a will or the intervention of southern legal institutions escaped scrutiny. The cases described here, then, are only a small part of a greater phenomenon.

Case Indexes

Cases are arranged per their appearance in the text.

CHAPTER ONE
Righteous Fathers, Vulnerable Old Men, and Degraded Creatures

Le Grand v. Darnall, 27 U.S. 664 (1829).

Hamilton v. Cragg, 6 Harris & Johns. 16 (Md., 1823).

Hall v. Mullin, 5 Harris & Johns. 190 (Md., 1821).

Bates v. Holman, 13 Va. 202 (1809).

Foster's Administrator v. Fosters, 51 Va. 485 (1853).

Dunlop & als. v. Harrison's Executors & als., 55 Va. 251 (1858).

Greenlow v. Rawlings, 22 Tenn. 90 (1842).

Hubbard's Will, 29 Ky. 58 (1831).

Narcissa's Executors v. Wathan et al., 41 Ky. 241 (1842).

Campbell v. Campbell, 13 Ark. 513 (1853).

Davis v. Calvert, 5 G. &. J. 269 (Md., 1833).

Denton v. Franklin, 48 Ky. 28 (1848).

Ford v. Ford, 26 Tenn. 92 (1846).

Pool's Heirs v. Pool's Executor, 33 Ala. 145 (1858).

Pool's Heirs v. Pool's Executor, 35 Ala. 12 (1859).

Farr v. Thompson, Executor of Farr, Cheves 37 (S.C., 1839).

Jolliffe v. Fanning, 10 Richardson 186 (S.C., 1856).

Thomas D. Bennehan's Ex'qr v. John Norwood, Ex'qr & al., 40 N.C. 106 (1847).

Green v. Lane, 45 N.C. 102 (1852).

Lucy Thomas and others v. Nathaniel J. Palmer, 54 N.C. 249 (1854).

Cunningham's Heirs v. Cunningham's Ex'rs, 1 N.C. 519 (1801).

Carmille v. Adm'r of Carmille et al., 2 McMullan 454 (S.C., 1842).

Broughton v. Telfer, 3 Rich. Eq. 431, 438 (S.C., 1851).

Mallet v. Smith, 6 Rich. Eq. 12, 20 (S.C., 1852).

CHAPTER TWO

Slavery, Freedom, and the Rule of Law

Mutual Protection Insurance Co. v. Hamilton and Goram, 37 Tenn. 269
    (1857).
Cooper v. Blakely, 10 Ga. 263 (1851).
Sanders v. Ward, 25 Ga. 109 (1858).
Drane v. Beall, 21 Ga. 21 (1857).
Cleland v. Waters, 16 Ga. 496 (1854).
Vance v. Crawford, 4 Ga. 445 (1848).
Bryan v. Walton, 33 Ga. Supp. 11 (1864).
Hinds v. Brazealle et al., 3 Miss. 837 (1838).
Barksdale v. Elam, 30 Miss. 694 (1856).
Shaw v. Brown, 35 Miss. 246 (1858).
Mitchell v. Wells, 37 Miss. 235 (1859).
Bore's Ex'r v. Quierry's Ex'r, 4 Mart. (o.s.) 545 (Louisiana, 1816).
Tonnelier v. Maurin's Ex'r, 2 Mart. (o.s.) 206 (Superior Court First District,
    Louisiana, 1812).
Compton v. Prescott, 12 Rob. 56 (Louisiana, 1845).
Executors of Hart v. Boni (f.w.c.), 6 La. 97 (1838).
Dupre v. Uzee, 6 La. Ann. 280 (1851).
Lopez's Heirs v. Mary Bergel (f.w.c.), 12 La. 197 (1838).
Macarty v. Mandeville, 3 La. Ann. 239 (1848).
Badillo v. Tio, 6 La. Ann. 129 (1851).
Vail v. Bird, 6 La. Ann. 223 (1851).
Hardesty v. Wormley, 10 La. 239 (1855).
Adams v. Routh and Dorsey, 8 La. Ann. 121 (1853).
Virginia and Celesie, f.p.c., v. D. and C. Himel, 10 La. Ann. 185 (1855).
Pigeau v. Duvenay, 4 Mart. (o.s.) 266 (Louisiana, 1816).
Robinett v. Verdun's Vendees, 14 La. 542 (1840).
Jung v. Doriocourt, 4 La. 175 (1831).
Courcelle's Syndic v. Vitry (f.w.c.), 15 La. Ann. 653 (1860).
Prevost v. Martel, 10 Rob. 512 (La., 1845).

Opinions on the Emancipation of Slaves during George Robertson's Tenure as Chief Justice

George Robertson joined the Kentucky Court of Appeals in 1828 and served as chief justice from 1829 until 1842 (represented by GR below). Samuel S. Nicholas served from 1831 to 1834 (SSN). Ephraim M. Ewing joined the court in 1835 (EME), as did Thomas A. Marshall (TAM). Listed here in chronological order, these opinions were "opinions of the court" in that there were no dissents.

GR. *Conclude v. Williams*, 24 Ky. 16 (1829).

GR. *Joe v. Hart's Executors*, 25 Ky. 349 (1829).

GR. *Ferguson et al. v. Sarah et al.*, 27 Ky. 103 (1830).

GR. *Beaty v. Judy*, 31 Ky. 101 (1833).

SSN. *Young v. Slaughter*, 32 Ky. 384 (1834).

GR. *Barringtons v. Logan's Administrators*, 32 Ky. 432 (1834).

GR. *Gentry v. McMinnis*, 33 Ky. 382 (1835).

GR. *Black v. Meaux*, 34 Ky. 188 (1836).

GR. *Boyce v. Nancy*, 34 Ky. 236 (1836).

GR. *Aleck v. Tevis*, 34 Ky. 242 (1836).

GR. *Catherine Bodine's Will*, 34 Ky. 476 (1836).

GR. *Hudgens v. Spencer*, 34 Ky. 589 (1836).

GR. *Jameson v. Emaline*, 35 Ky. 207 (1837).

GR. *Howard v. Samples*, 35 Ky. 306

EME. *Susan (a colored woman) v. Ladd*, 36 Ky. 30 (1837).

EME. *Nancy (a colored woman) v. Snell*, 36 Ky. 148 (1838).

GR. *Dunlap and Collins v. Archer*, 37 Ky. 30 (1838).

TAM. *Hundley v. Perry*, 37 Ky. 359 (1838).

GR. *Craig v. McMullin*, 39 Ky. 311 (1840).

GR. *Jones v. John Bennet and Samuel Bennet*, 39 Ky. 333 (1840).

TAM. *Snead v. David*, 39 Ky. 350 (1840).

GR. *Caleb v. Field et al.*, 39 Ky. 346 (1840).

GR. *Thomas v. Beckman*, 40 Ky. 29 (1840).

GR. *Chancellor v. Milton*, 40 Ky. 25 (1840).

GR. *White's Heirs v. Turner*, 40 Ky. 130 (1840).

GR. *Narcissa's Executors v. Wathan et al.*, 41 Ky. 241 (1842).

GR. *Esther et al. v. Akins' heirs*, 42 Ky. 60 (1842).

Supplementary Information Regarding Willis v. Jolliffe

Of the fifty men signing the petition in 1860, not all of their signatures could be deciphered. One can get a sense of who they were, however, by referring to census records. Doing so poses its own problems of deciphering handwritten records written by government officials who interviewed residents of local communities, sometimes relying on hearsay and secondhand information in drafting their records. Thus discrepancies and ambiguities can be found. Nonetheless, census records are often the best sources available. The following were used: *Manuscript Census Returns, Seventh Census of the United States, 1850, Barnwell County, South Carolina,* National Archives Microform Series M-432, roll 849, Manuscript Census Returns, *Eighth Census of the United States, 1860, Barnwell County, South Carolina,* National Archives Microform Series M-653, roll 1213; National Archives Microform Series M-432 1099 rolls, *1850 Slave Census;* National Archives Microform Series M-653, 1438 rolls, *1860 Slave Census;* and the on-line census database, <www.ancestry.com>.

Among the signers of the petition were slave-owning planters, farmers, and merchants. The men's slave-owning status in 1860 follows by employment category per the 1860 census.

Planters: Johnson Hagood, a planter and the commissioner in equity, owning 23 slaves; William Armstrong, owning 16 slaves in Abbeville; Wm. Walker, owning 3 slaves in Colleton; James Riley, owning 3 slaves in Abbeville; William Mathews, owning 20 slaves in Colleton. The rest were listed as owning slaves in Barnwell: B. H. Brown, owning 13 slaves; J. M. Hutto (who might have been a sheriff in 1860), owning 10 slaves; E. L. Patterson, owning 12 slaves; John Aaron, owning about 80 slaves; W. P. Dunbar, owning 49 slaves; Jno. E. Tobin, owning 20 slaves; James Furse, owning 38 slaves. Farmers: Jesse Miller, owning 8 slaves; Drury Sprawls, owning 19 slaves; Edwin Stansell, owning 6 slaves; Owen R. Faust, owning 35 slaves. B. F. Peebles, a planter-merchant, owned 40 slaves. The farmer G. W. Askue and the merchant A. P. Bogacki owned no slaves. The merchants C. C. Cooper and J. G. Googe owned 8 and 4 slaves, respectively. It is unclear whether Peter Carson, R. M. Mims, H. Asher, and G. E. Voney owned any slaves.

Angus Patterson's identity is somewhat ambiguous. In 1850 Angus Patterson was sixty-four years old, a contemporary of Willis, a planter worth $30,000 and the head of his household. He signed the certificate of good character given to Willis when he was planning on taking Amy and the children to Maryland. But in 1860 there appeared to be two men named Angus Patterson living in Barnwell. One, whose age was not listed, appeared to be the one found in the 1850 census; he was worth $117,200 but living in the household of E. L. Patterson, a thirty-seven-year-old planter worth $41,200.

Living nearby was another Angus Patterson, twenty-three years old in 1860 and worth $2,000, though nothing else is definitely known about him. E. L. Patterson—also known as Edward Lawrence—had a son, however, Angus Bethune Patterson, born in 1851, who later served in the state senate, representing Barnwell in the early twentieth century. He followed in the footsteps of his namesake grandfather, Angus Patterson, who served in the house of representatives from 1818 to 1812 and in the senate from 1822 to 1849, but who died in 1854. From N. Louise Bailey, Mary L. Morgan, and Carolyn R. Taylor., *Biographical Directory of the South Carolina Senate: 1776–1985* (Columbia: University of South Carolina Press, 1986), 1237–39.

If the records, dates, and ages are in conflict because of errors in record keeping, such as where the dead Angus Patterson appeared to have been listed as though he were alive, there in all likelihood could have been three men named Angus Patterson: the patriarch and former senator who died in 1854, his son Angus, the sibling of E.L., born in 1836 who lived with his brother, and the grandson born in 1851. Insofar as the census included the value of properties held by individual families, the deceased Angus Patterson's property might have been listed in 1860, but E.L. was managing the estate, which owned 172 slaves. In all likelihood it was the twenty-three-year-old Angus Patterson who signed the petition.

Several were lawyers and government officials who would have had knowledge of the community and legal proceedings taking place in the courts, combined with their access to the legislature. Johnson Hagood, commissioner in equity; R. C. Fowke, the ordinary for Barnwell; V. J. Williamson; J. L. Davis, clerk of the court; Wm. R. Halford, sheriff for Barnwell District; L. O'Bannon, magistrate; A. P. Aldrich; H. D. Duncan;

F. F. Dunbar; George W. Moye; and J. J. Ryan, who shared the same name with a J. J. Ryan who in the 1860s, was a Confederate official charged with confiscating the estates of disloyal southerners. The estate was seized at that time.

John B. Armstrong acted as assistant marshal in taking the census of 1860, living in Anderson and owning sixteen slaves; J. M. Hutson was a lawyer owning four slaves; J. W. Freeman worked in the court of the ordinary, the court assigned to handle trusts and estates matters. As mentioned in chapter 5, John M. Whetstone, another lawyer, submitted the petition on behalf of the group. He served as a member of the House of Representatives for Barnwell from 1860 to 1863. Freeman was forty-one in 1860; Hutson was about forty, and Whetstone, about twenty-three years old. Freeman was worth $1,500; Hutson, $600, and Whetstone, $500. As a comparison, the Willis estate was worth about $45,000, according to an 1855 inventory: Barnwell County Estate Papers, *Elijah Willis*, bundle 126, package 7.

THE BARNWELL COUNTY JUDGE OF PROBATE MANUMISSION BOOK

The Barnwell County Judge of Probate Manumission Book 1803–45 indicates the following manumissions. Andrew, a free Negro manumitted his wife and four children on April 22, 1803. William Williams freed Moses, a Negro man, in consideration of Moses's good conduct and a sum of $500 on June 3, 1803. On April 12, 1806, Isaac Bourdeaux emancipated his Negro woman slave, Philly, in consideration of ten shillings paid to him. He also freed Lincoln Bourdeaux, her son. George Bellinger freed Mary Cecilia, described by the certifying freeholders on October 16, 1810, as a female slave "who in the appearance of her eyes, features & complexion is in our opinion is not distinguishable from a white person." That same day Bellinger also freed Sarah, described as "a mulatto or half breed." Eliz. P. Townsend freed Molly three years later, on November 17, 1813. George Fisher freed Henry on December 11, 1813. George Bruton freed "in consideration of Sertain Services Emancipated and Set free a Sertain Negro Woman named Sarah," on September 21, 1815. A few weeks later Aquilly Bruton, Benjamin Bruton, and George Bruton also freed, in consideration of services, a Negro man named Jim. Benjamin Bowers sold his slave Vinter's freedom to him for $500 on August 9, 1817. "Free Moses" emancipated Sarah and Betty on November 19, 1817, in return for $1,000. Andrew McElmurray sold

Dick his freedom for $495. Stephen P. Floid was the last to free a slave under the law of 1800: Jacob Floid on August 10, 1820, in return for $500. Source: South Carolina Department of Archives and History.

RECORDS OF LAND SALES BY AMY ASH NÉE WILLIS FROM THE BARN-
WELL COUNTY CONVEYANCE BOOK, SOUTH CAROLINA DEPARTMENT
OF ARCHIVES AND HISTORY

Volume YY, p. 11–12 (1870), reel C5410: $400 worth of land. The sellers were "Amy Ash Clarissa A. L. Sloan (formerly Willis) Julia Willis and Elijah Willis, heirs and legatees" under Elijah Willis's will.
Volume ZZ, p. 628 (1871), reel C5411: $600 worth of land.
Volume AAA, p. 529 (1871), reel C5412: several tracts sold for $2,000.
Volume AAA, p. 530, reel C5412; land sold for $425.

For information on Amy in 1870, see Manuscript Census Returns, Ninth Census of the United States, 1870, Clermont County Ohio, Ohio Twp., National Archives Microform Series M-653, roll 944, p. 17.

One might wonder: how did Willis reconcile his ownership of Amy with his relationship to her as a member of his household? Perhaps Willis adhered to a benevolent, paternalistic model of slavery. Perhaps he thought treating her as a partner mitigated any criticism that he took advantage of her, or that he was an evil slave owner. Although the system of slavery had long been criticized by abolitionists as built upon exploitation and greed, it is possible that men like Willis could argue that even though others believed they acted purely out of base and selfish motives, their situations were far more nuanced. In treating their enslaved partners with the respect that would usually be given to a white woman, they were more "humane."

How did his intimate relationship with her begin? How did he resolve the conflicts in his children? He also owned Amy's older children, the darker ones who might not have been fathered by him. How did he treat them? Was his ownership of the entire family merely a formality, one that the law required, the only one that would be recognized? Did he see his ownership as the best means of making sure they were well taken care of, until he could make arrangements for them, arrangements he could not make within South Carolina? Did he see his payment of any taxes owed on them as merely incidental to their upkeep? Granted, he freed them by bringing them to Ohio, but he kept records of his ownership. How else could the assessor have listed Amy and the children as being worth $1,400? Had he bought her? Had she been a gift from Kirkland? The record does not indicate, and the complexity of the situation raises more questions than answers.

As for Amy, it is unclear how she felt. Did she feel resentment at the race-based, gender-based, and caste-based oppressions of southern law that limited her possibilities and that would deny her a rightful inheritance? Was she hiding away in Ohio, fearful for her life, that she might be dragged back into slavery? How did she feel about Willis? Did she feel affection, or did she merely tolerate him? Was she a woman trying to make the best of her situation? Had she and Willis made an arrangement that they would live together? Had Willis told her of what he was trying to do in order to free her and the children, to make sure they received an inheritance? Living with Willis as his partner, gaining benefits through that status, even though she was a slave, did other slaves feel resentful of her? Did she feel superior to them?

By an act of 1740 all blacks of full African descent or mixed "were absolute slaves forever, personal chattels; condition to follow the mother."[1] The mixed-race child of a white woman was "a mulatto, within the meaning of that term . . . subject to all the disabilities of the degraded caste, into which his color thrusts him."[2] But because his mother was white he was free.

What this meant is that a black woman like Amy was a slave for life, unless manumitted. Her children inherited her slave status, not the status of their white father. If she as a slave woman believed her rights had been violated, she had no recourse because a violation against her as a matter of law was seen as a violation against her owner instead: it was up to the owner to pursue "the prosecution of those rights."[3] An owner who took advantage of his female slave was thus practicably immune from prosecution. Moreover, as the legislature's failure to act upon the Barnwell petition indicates, no authorities prosecuted owners for living "in open connection" with female slaves.

NOTES

INTRODUCTION
Inheritance Rights in the Antebellum South

1. On the application of the law of slavery to reinforce the slave order see for example, Mark Tushnet, *The American Law of Slavery: Considerations of Humanity and Interest: 1810–1860* (Princeton, N.J.: Princeton University Press, 1981), for Tushnet's view of the slave regime requiring racial hegemony as the foundation for its economic order.

2. Thomas D. Morris, *Southern Slavery and the Law: 1619–1860* (Chapel Hill: University of North Carolina Press, 1996), 13.

3. William E. Wiethoff, *A Peculiar Humanism: The Judicial Advocacy of Slavery in High Courts of the Old South, 1820–1850* (Athens: University of Georgia Press, 1996), 12–13.

4. Adrienne D. Davis, "Slavery and the Roots of Sexual Harassment," in Catharine A. MacKinnon and Reva Siegel, eds., *Directions in Sexual Harassment Law* (New Haven: Yale University Press, 2004), 457–78.

5. Ariela J. Gross, *Double Character: Slavery and Mastery in the Antebellum Southern Courtroom* (Princeton, N.J.: Princeton University Press, 2000).

6. Mark Tushnet, *The American Law of Slavery: Considerations of Humanity and Interest: 1810–1860* (Princeton, N.J.: Princeton University Press, 1981).

7. See Robert Samuel Summers, *Instrumentalism and American Legal Theory* (Ithaca, N.Y.: Cornell University Press, 1982); Frederick Schauer, "Formalism," 97 *Yale Law Journal* 509 (1988).

8. Bernie D. Jones, "Southern Free Women of Color in the Antebellum North: Race, Class and a 'New Women's Legal History,'" 41 *University of Akron Law Review* 763 (2008).

9. Patricia Ewick and Susan S. Silbey, *The Common Place of Law: Stories from Everyday Life* (Chicago: University of Chicago Press, 1998), 35.

10. Judith Kelleher Schafer, *Becoming Free, Remaining Free: Manumission and Enslavement in New Orleans, 1856–1862* (Baton Rouge: Louisiana State University Press, 2003).

CHAPTER ONE

Righteous Fathers, Vulnerable Old Men, and Degraded Creatures

1. Robert Weisberg, "Proclaiming Trials as Narratives: Premises and Pretensions," in Peter Brooks and Paul Gewirtz, eds., *Law's Stories: Narrative and Rhetoric in the Law* (New Haven: Yale University Press, 1996), 66.

2. Ibid.

3. Morris, *Southern Slavery and the Law*, 321.

4. Ibid., 372.

5. *Le Grand v. Darnall*, 27 U.S. 664 (1829).

6. Ibid., 668.

7. *Hamilton v. Cragg*, 6 Harris & Johns. 16 (Md., 1823), was the case involving the manumission of the three-year-old. *Le Grand v. Darnall*, 27 U.S. 664, 668 (1829).

8. *Le Grand v. Darnall*, 27 U.S. 669 (1829).

9. Ibid., 670.

10. *Le Grand v. Darnall*, 27 U.S. 664, 668 (1829), referring to *Hall v. Mullin*, 5 Harris & Johns. 190 (Md., 1821).

11. *Bates v. Holman*, 13 Va. 202 (1809).

12. Ibid., 540.

13. *Foster's Administrator v. Fosters*, 51 Va. 485, 486 (1853).

14. Ibid., 487.

15. Ibid., 491.

16. *Dunlop & als. V. Harrison's Executors & als.*, 55 Va. 251, 258 (1858), referring to Virginia Code, ch. 104, § 4, p. 458 (1832).

17. Ibid., 260–61.

18. Ibid. 259.

19. Ibid., 267.

20. Ibid., 263.

21. *Greenlow v. Rawlings*, 22 Tenn. 90 (1842).

22. Ibid., 92.

23. Ibid., 91.

24. Ibid., 3.

25. *Hubbard's Will*, 29 Ky. 58, 60 (1831).

26. Ibid.

27. *Narcissa's Executors v. Wathan et al.*, 41 Ky. 241 (1842).

28. Ibid.

29. Ibid. 243.

30. Ibid.

31. *Campbell v. Campbell*, 13 Ark. 513, 517 (1853).

32. Ibid.

33. Ibid.

34. Ibid.

35. Ibid.

36. Ibid., 519.

37. Ibid.

38. *Davis v. Calvert*, 5 G. & J. 269 (Md., 1833).

39. 5 G. & J. 269, 307.

40. Ibid., 307.

41. *Denton v. Franklin*, 48 Ky. 28, 30 (1848).

42. Ibid.

43. *Ford v. Ford*, 26 Tenn. 92, 102 (1846).

44. Ibid., 102, 103.

45. Arthur F. Howington, "'Not in the Condition of a Horse or an Ox': *Ford v. Ford*, The Law of Testamentary Manumission, and the Tennessee Courts' Recognition of Slave Humanity," 34 *Tennessee Historical Quarterly* 249–63 (1975).

46. *Ford v. Ford*, 95, 96.

47. Wiethoff, *Peculiar Humanism*, 45.

48. Ibid., 97.

49. See *Greenlow v. Rawlings*, 22 Tenn. 90 (1842).

50. *Pool's Heirs v. Pool's Executor*, 33 Ala. 145 (1858).

51. *Pool's Heirs v. Pool's Executor*, 35 Ala. 12, 17 (1859).

52. *Farr v. Thompson, Executor of Farr*, Cheves 37, 38 (S.C., 1839).

53. Ibid.

54. Ibid., 40.

55. Ibid., 41.

56. Ibid., 40.

57. Ibid., 42.

58. Ibid., 46.

59. Ibid., 47.

60. Ibid., 48.

61. Ibid., 49.

62. *Jolliffe v. Fanning*, 10 Richardson 186, 187 (S.C., 1856).

63. Ibid., 192.

64. Ibid.

65. Ibid., 199–200.

66. Ibid., 195.

67. Ibid., 200.

68. Ibid., 201.

69. Gross, *Double Character.*

CHAPTER TWO
Slavery, Freedom, and the Rule of Law

1. See Feldman, *American Legal Thought from Premodernism to Postmodernism.*

2. *Cunningham's Heirs v. Cunningham's Ex'rs,* 1 N.C. 519 (1801).

3. Ibid.

4. *Thomas D. Bennehan's Ex'qr v. John Norwood, Ex'qr & al.,* 40 N.C. 106 (1847).

5. Ibid.

6. Ibid.

7. *Cunningham,* 521.

8. *Green v. Lane,* 45 N.C. 102 (1852).

9. See Wiethoff, *Peculiar Humanism,* 87.

10. *Green v. Lane,* 112.

11. *Lucy Thomas and others v. Nathaniel J. Palmer,* 54 N.C. 249 (1854).

12. Ibid.

13. Ibid.

14. Ibid., 251.

15. Ibid., 252.

16. *Carmille v. Adm'r of Carmille et al.,* 2 McMullan 454 (S.C., 1842).

17. Ibid., 455.

18. Ibid., 466.

19. Ibid., 469.

20. South Carolina Department of Archives and History, Records of the General Assembly, John Carmille petition, n.d., no. 1807 (submitted to the senate 27 Nov. 1821).

21. Ibid.

22. Ibid.

23. *Broughton v. Telfer,* 3 Rich. Eq. 431, 438 (S.C., 1851).

24. *Mallet v. Smith,* 6 Rich. Eq. 12, 20 (S.C., 1852).

25. Ibid., 13.

26. Ibid., 25.

27. *Mutual Protection Insurance Co. v. Hamilton and Goram*, 37 Tenn. 269 (1857).

28. Ibid., 272.

29. Ibid., 275.

30. Ibid., 278.

31. *Cooper v. Blakely*, 10 Ga. 263 (1851).

32. *Sanders v. Ward*, 25 Ga. 109, 124 (1858).

33. See for example *Drane v. Beall*, 21 Ga. 21 (1857).

34. *Cleland v. Waters*, 16 Ga. 496, 517 (1854).

35. *Vance v. Crawford*, 4 Ga. 445, 459 (1848).

36. *Bryan v. Walton*, 33 Ga. Supp. 11, 24 (1864).

37. Ibid., 25.

38. *Hinds v. Brazealle et al.*, 3 Miss. 837, 838 (1838).

39. Finkelman, *An Imperfect Union*, 285–93.

40. *Hinds v. Brazealle*, 3 Miss. 837, 841 (1838).

41. Ibid.

42. Ibid., 843.

43. *Barksdale v. Elam*, 30 Miss. 694 (1856).

44. Ibid., 697.

45. *Shaw v. Brown*, 35 Miss. 246, 248 (1858).

46. Ibid., 319.

47. Ibid., 315.

48. *Mitchell v. Wells*, 37 Miss. 235, 237 (1859).

49. Ibid., 237.

50. Ibid., 252.

51. Ibid.

52. de Tocqueville, *Journey to America*, 100.

53. Ibid.

54. Ibid.

55. Ibid., 165.

56. *Tonnelier v. Maurin's Ex'r*, 2 Mart. (o.s.) 206 (Superior Court First District, La., 1812).

57. *Courcelle's Syndic v. Vitry (f.w.c.)*, 15 La. An. 653 (1860).

58. *Bore's Ex'r v. Quierry's Ex'r*, 4 Mart. (o.s.) 545, 551 (La., 1816).

59. Ibid., 554.

60. *Compton v. Prescott*, 12 Rob. 56, 69 (La., 1845).

61. *Executors of Hart v. Boni (f.w.c.)*, 6 La. 97, 98, 99 (1838).

62. *Dupre v. Uzee*, 6 La. Ann. 280 (1851).

63. *Lopez's Heirs v. Mary Bergel (f.w.c.)*, 12 La. 197, 201 (1838).

64. *Macarty v. Mandeville*, 3 La. Ann. 239, 240 (1848).

65. Ibid., 244.

66. Ibid., 245.

67. *Badillo v. Tio*, 6 La. Ann. 129 (1851).

68. *Vail v. Bird*, 6 La. Ann. 223 (1851).

69. Ibid., 224.

70. Cobb, *Inquiry into the Law of Negro Slavery*, 83.

71. Ibid., 100.

72. Ibid.

73. *Hardesty v. Wormley*, 10 La. 239 (1855).

74. Ibid.

75. Ibid., 240.

76. Ibid.

77. Ibid.

78. *Adams v. Routh and Dorsey*, 8 La. Ann. 121 (1853).

79. *Virginia and Celesie, f.p.c., v. D. and C. Himel*, 10 La. An. 185 (1855).

80. *Adams v. Routh and Dorsey*, 121 (1843).

81. *Pigeau v. Duvenay*, 4 Mart. (o.s.) 266 (La., 1816). See also *Robinett v. Verdun's Vendees*, 14 La. 542 (1840).

82. *Jung v. Doriocourt*, 4 La. 175, 178 (1831).

83. Ibid.

84. Martin biographical information in Wiethoff, 150. Quotation in *Jung v. Doriocourt*, 179.

85. *Badillo v. Tio*, 138.

86. Ibid.

87. See e.g., *Prevost v. Martel*, 10 Rob. 512 (La., 1845); *Compton v. Prescott*, 12 Rob. 56 (La., 1845).

88. *Badillo v. Tio*, 138.

CHAPTER THREE
Justice and Mercy in the Kentucky Court of Appeals

1. One such case was *Catherine Bodine's Will*, 34 Ky. 476, 477 (1836), a case in which Jenny and others of the late Bodine's slaves brought in to court a document they claimed was her will; Robertson, writing for the Court of Appeals of Kentucky, reversed the lower court opinion holding the will was invalid.

2. 1880, Louisville, Jefferson, Ky., roll T9_424, www.Ancestry.com; family history film 1254424, p. 183.2000, enumeration district 141, image 0088.

3. Narcissa's will, Nelson County Will, book 2, p. 22, Nelson County Clerk's Office.

4. *Narcissa's Executors v. Wathan et al.*, 41 Ky. 241 (1842).

5. *Hubbard's Will*, 29 Ky. 58 (1831).

6. Ibid., 59.

7. *Reed's Will*, 41 Ky. 79, 80 (1841).

8. Ibid.

9. Nelson County Order book D, November 1847–October 1853, p. 19–20, 14 Feb. 1848 entry, Nelson County Clerk's Office.

10. William Draper Lewis, *Great American Lawyers: A History of the Legal Profession in America* (Philadelphia: John C. Winston, 1908), 4: 387. Other justices who served with Robertson during the antebellum period include Joseph Underwood, Ephraim M. Ewing, Thomas A. Marshall, and Samuel S. Nicholas. Joseph Underwood sat on the bench from 1828 to 1835. He was a congressman from 1835 to 1843 and 1847 to 1853. As one of the "antislavery colonizationists," he believed slaves in the United States should be emancipated and repatriated to Africa. Ephraim M. Ewing joined the court in 1835 and served as chief justice from 1843 to 1846, until he left the bench. Thomas A. Marshall served from 1835 to 1856, as chief justice from 1847 to 1851 and 1854 to 1856. Samuel S. Nicholas served from 1831 to 1834. Harold D. Tallant, *Evil Necessity: Slavery and Political Culture in Antebellum Kentucky* (Lexington: University Press of Kentucky, 2003), 40; <http://library.louisville.edu/law/Research/KyHiCt.htm>.

11. See appendix 2 for a list of cases.

12. *Narcissa's Executors v. Wathan et al.*, 41 Ky. 241, 243 (1842).

13. Robert I. Vexler, *Chronology and Documentary Handbook of the State of Kentucky* (Dobbs Ferry, N.Y.: Oceana Publications, 1978), 94.

14. Victor B. Howard, *The Evangelical War against Slavery and Caste: The Life and Times of John G. Fee* (Selinsgrove, Pa.: Susquehanna University Press, 1996), 13, 14, 17.

15. Vexler, *Chronology*, 20.

16. Ibid., 17, 18. For general histories of Kentucky in the antebellum period, see for example Ivan E. McDougle, *Slavery in Kentucky* (Westport, Conn.: Negro Universities Press, 1970); Asa Earl Martin, *The Anti-Slavery Movement in Kentucky, Prior to 1850* (Westport, Conn.: Negro Universities Press, 1970); H. Edward Richardson, *Cassius Marcellus Clay: Firebrand of Freedom* (Lexington: University Press of Kentucky, 1976); Maurice G. Baxter, *Henry Clay and the American System* (Lexington: University Press of Kentucky, 1995); and Tallant, *Evil Necessity*.

17. Michael F. Holt, *The Rise and Fall of the American Whig Party: Jacksonian Politics and the Onset of the Civil War* (New York: Oxford University Press, 1999), 81.

18. Ibid., 118.

19. William Littell, esq., *The Statute Law of Kentucky: With Notes, Praelections, and Observations on the Public Acts*, vol. 2 (Frankfort, Ky.: printed for William Hunter, by Johnston and Pleasants, 1810), ch. 63, § 27, p. 113), Kentucky Department of Archives and Libraries.

20. Ibid.

21. Ibid., § 37, p. 121.

22. Morris, *Southern Slavery and the Law*, 61–80.

23. *Winney v. Cartright*, 10 Ky. 493, 495 (1821).

24. *Cooke v. Cooke*, 13 Ky. 238, 239 (1823).

25. *Innes v. Lyne's Devisees*, 2 Ky. 299, 300 (1803).

26. Ibid.

27. Ibid.

28. *Thompson v. Wilmot*, 4 Ky. 422 (1809).

29. Ibid., 423.

30. Ibid., 424.

31. Ibid.

32. *Leah et al. v. Young and Shackleford*, 12 Ky. 18 (1829).

33. George Robertson, "Introductory Lecture, Delivered in the chapel of Morrison College," *Scrap book on Law, Politics, Men and Times* (Lexington, Ky.: A. W. Elder, 1855), 182, Kentucky Historical Society, University of Kentucky Library. Hereafter cited as Morrison College address.

34. *White's Heirs v. Turner*, 40 Ky. 130 (1840).

35. Ibid.

36. Ibid.

37. Ibid., 131.

38. Ibid.

39. *Dunlap and Collins v. Archer*, 37 Ky. 30, 35–36 (1838).

40. Robertson, Morrison College address, 183.

41. *Patton's Heirs v. Patton's Executors*, 28 Ky. 389–90 (1831).

42. *Young v. Slaughter*, 32 Ky. 384 (1834).

43. Ibid.

44. Ibid., 385.

45. Ibid.

46. Ibid.

47. Ibid.

48. *Gentry v. McMinnis*, 33 Ky. 382 (1835).

49. *Joe v. Hart's Executors*, 25 Ky. 249 (1829).

50. Ibid., 350.

51. Ibid.

52. *Conclude v. Williamson*, 24 Ky. 16, 18 (1829).

53. Ibid., 16.

54. Ibid., 20.

55. *Ferguson et al. v. Sarah et al.*, 27 Ky. 103 (1830).

56. Ibid., 104.

57. *Black v. Meaux*, 34 Ky. 188 (1836).

58. Ibid., 189.

59. *Aleck v. Tevis*, 34 Ky. 242, 244 (1836).

60. *Nancy (a colored woman) v. Snell*, 36 Ky. 148, 149 (1838).

61. Ibid.

62. *Snead v. David*, 39 Ky. 350, 355–56 (1840).

63. *Boyce v. Nancy*, 34 Ky. 236, 240 (1836).

64. *Jameson v. Emaline*, 35 Ky. 207, 209 (1837).

65. Robertson, Morrison College address, 172.

66. Robertson, "Address on Behalf of the Deinologian Society," *Scrap Book*, 164, Kentucky Historical Society, University of Kentucky Library.

67. Tallant, *Evil Necessity*, 3–5.

68. Robertson, "Speech on the bill to modify the law of 1833," *Scrap Book*, 322.

69. Ibid.

70. Ibid., 323.

71. Ibid., 323.

72. Robertson, Morrison College address, 173.

73. Robertson, speaking of himself in the third person in "Speech on the bill to modify the law of 1833," *Scrap Book*, 323–24.

74. Howard, *Evangelical War*, 18.

75. Ibid., 46.

76. See for example Thomas Morris, *Southern Slavery and the Law*, 371–423.

77. *Wood's Executors v. Wickliffe*, 44 Ky. 187, 191–92 (1844).

78. *Commonwealth v. Stout*, 46 Ky. 247 (1847).

79. Ibid., 248.

80. *Mullins v. Wall*, 47 Ky. 445, 448 (1848).

81. *Orchard v. David (a free man of color)*, 45 Ky. 376, 378 (1846).

82. *Darcus v. Crump*, 45 Ky. 363, 365 (1846).

83. Ibid., 368.

84. *Acts of the General Assembly of the Commonwealth of Kentucky 1840*, ch. 257, §§ 1–3 (Frankfort, Ky.: A. G. Hodges, 1841), 41, Kentucky Department of Archives and Libraries.

85. On slaves being entitled to the monies obtained through their hire, see ibid., ch. 257, §§ 4–5, p. 42. On slaves not becoming public charges, see *Acts of the General Assembly of the Commonwealth of Kentucky 1841*, ch. 92 (Frankfort, Ky.: A. G. Hodges, State Printer, 1842), 20, Kentucky Department of Archives and Libraries.

86. *Hill v. Squire*, 51 Ky. 557 (1851).

87. Ibid., 558.

88. Ibid.

89. Ibid., 558–59.

90. Ibid., 561.

91. Ibid.

92. *Major v. Winn's Adm'r*, 52 Ky. 250, 251 (1852).

93. Ibid., 251.

94. *Hawkins v. Hawkins*, 52 Ky. 245 (1852).

95. *Norris (of color) v. Patton's Adm'r*, 54 Ky. 575 (1855).

96. *Jones v. Lipscomb*, 53 Ky. 239 (1853).

97. *Anderson et al. v. Crawford*, 54 Ky. 328 (1854).

98. *Acts of the General Assembly passed at November session, 1850*, vol. 1, *Constitution of 1850*, art. 10, § 1 (Frankfort, Ky.: A. G. Hodges, 1851), 27, Kentucky Department of Archives and Libraries.

99. *Smith v. Adam*, 57 Ky. 685, 688 (1857).

100. *Acts of the General Assembly of the Commonwealth of Kentucky 1841*, ch. 92 (Frankfort, Ky.: A. G. Hodges, 1842), 20, Kentucky Department of Archives and Libraries.

101. *Smith v. Adam*, 690.

102. *Constitution of 1850*, art. 10, § 2 p. 28.

103. Figures for 1830: U.S. Census Office, *Abstract of the Returns of the Fifth Census, 1830* (Washington, D.C.: Duff & Green, 1832), 27. Figures for 1840: U.S. Census Office, *Sixth Census of 1840: Enumeration of Inhabitants* (Washington, D.C.: Blair & Rives, 1841), 288. Figures for 1860: U.S. Census Office, *Eighth Census of 1860* (Washington, D.C.: Government Printing Office, 1864), 179.

104. *Constitution of 1850*, art. 10, § 1.

105. *Jackson v. Collins*, 55 Ky. 214 (1855).

106. *Kitty v. Commonwealth,* 57 Ky. 522, 526 (1857).

107. Ibid., 527.

108. *Davis v. Reeves,* 58 Ky. 589, 590 (1859).

109. Ibid., 592.

CHAPTER FOUR

Circling the Wagons and Clamping Down:
The Mississippi High Court of Errors and Appeals

1. Paul Finkelman, *An Imperfect Union: Slavery, Federalism and Comity* (Clark, N.J.: Lawbook Exchange, 2000); Mark V. Tushnet, *The American Law of Slavery, 1810–1860: Considerations of Humanity and Interest* (Princeton, N.J.: Princeton University Press, 1981).

2. *Mitchell v. Wells* (Chancery, 1857) (order granting damages), 221, Mississippi Department of Archives and History, hereafter MDAH.

3. 1850, Columbus Ward 1, Lowndes, Miss., roll M432_376, p. 113, image 225, 1850 U.S. Federal Census—Slave Schedules, www.Ancestry.com.

4. 1850, Madison, Miss., roll M432_376, p. 145, image 289, 1850 U.S. Federal Census—Slave Schedules, www.Ancestry.com.

5. Rowland Dunbar, *Encyclopedia of Mississippi History,* vol. 1 (Southern Historical Association, 1916), 843, MDAH.

6. See for example 1 Jan. 1861, Speech of the Honorable A. H. Handy, Commissioner to Maryland from the State of Mississippi, delivered at Princess Anne (Jackson: Mississippi Book and Job Printing Office, 1861), Maryland Historical Society.

7. Thomas D. Morris, *American National Biography,* vol. 10, eds. John A. Garraty and Mark C. Carnes (New York: Oxford University Press, 1999), 4; Dunbar, *Encyclopedia,* 843.

8. Act of June 18, 1822, *Slaves,* § 75, 1822 Miss. Laws 198, MDAH.

9. Ibid., § 80 and 81.

10. Resolution of 3 Feb. 1825, ch. 76, 1825 Miss. Laws 145, MDAH.

11. Resolution of 23 Jan. 1826, ch. 85, 1826 Miss. Laws 125, MDAH.

12. Resolution of 27 Feb. 1836, 1836 Miss. Laws 101, MDAH.

13. Act of 20 Dec. 1831, ch. 5, § 1, 1831 Miss. Laws 10, MDAH.

14. Ibid.

15. Miss. Const., *Slaves,* § 1 (1832), MDAH.

16. Act of 26 Feb. 1842, ch. 4, § 2, 1842 Miss. Laws 66, MDAH.

17. Ibid., § 1.

18. Report of 6 March 1850, ch. 352, 1850 Miss. Laws 521, MDAH.

19. *Journal of the Convention of the State of Mississippi* (Jackson: Thomas Farmer, 1851), 1–20, MDAH.

20. Resolution of 12 March 1856, ch. 252, 1856 Miss. Laws 431, MDAH.

21. Petition of William Johnson, MDAH.

22. *Journal of the House of Representatives of the State of Mississippi* (Natchez: Richard C. Langdon, 1820), 73, 107, MDAH.

23. *Journal of the Senate of the State of Mississippi* (Natchez: Richard C. Langdon, 1820), 79, 118, MDAH.

24. Ibid., 104.

25. Petition of Louise Favre, MDAH.

26. *Journal of the House of Representatives of the State of Mississippi* (Columbia: Peter Isler, 1821), 22, 28, 33, 39, MDAH.

27. *Journal of the Senate of the State of Mississippi* (Columbia: Peter Isler, 1821), 37, 42, MDAH.

28. Jacques Andres petition, MDAH.

29. Ibid.

30. *Journal of the House of Representatives of the State of Mississippi* (Jackson: Peter Isler, 1826), 29, 37, 53, 80–81, MDAH.

31. Ibid., 50.

32. Petition of Jane Collins, MDAH.

33. *Journal of the House of Representatives of the State of Mississippi* (Jackson: Peter Isler, 1833), 330, MDAH.

34. Ibid., 149.

35. *Journal of the House of Representatives of the State of Mississippi* (Jackson: George R. Fall, 1833), 198, MDAH.

36. Act of 21 Jan. 1833, ch. 43, 1833 Miss. Laws 119, MDAH.

37. Act of 23 Jan. 1833, ch. 50, 1833 Miss. Laws 125, MDAH.

38. Act of 16 Feb. 1844, ch. 175, 1844 Miss. Laws 354–55, MDAH.

39. Resolution on behalf of Esther Barland, MDAH.

40. Act of 24 Dec. 1814, 1814 Miss Laws 40, MDAH.

41. Petition of Andrew Barland, MDAH.

42. Thomas R. R. Cobb, *An Inquiry into the Law of Negro Slavery* (Philadelphia: T. & J. W. Johnson & Co., 1858), 312.

43. Act of 18 June 1822, Slaves, § 76, 1822 Miss. Laws 198, MDAH.

44. *Hinds v. Brazealle*, 3 Miss. 837 (1838).

45. Ibid.

46. Ibid., 847.

47. *Shaw v. Brown*, 355 Miss. 246 (1858).

48. William L. Harris, *Address Before the Agricultural Association, Jackson, November 12, 1858* (Jackson, Mississippi: E. Barksdale, 1858), 11, MDAH.

49. Ibid., 19–20.

50. Complaint at 7, *Mitchell v. Wells* (Chancery, 1857), MDAH.

51. Ibid., 8.

52. Ibid., 11.

53. Ibid., Edward Wells last will and testament, 12.

54. Ibid., Patrick Henry deposition, 117.

55. Ibid., Hannah Dudley deposition, 101.

56. Ibid.

57. Ibid.

58. Ibid., Alan Taylor deposition, 110.

59. Ibid., Francis Mitchell deposition, 90.

60. Ibid., William Mitchell answer, 32.

61. Ibid., 33.

62. Ibid., Francis Mitchell deposition, 76.

63. Ibid., John R. Lambeth deposition, 74.

64. Ibid., Francis Mitchell deposition, 81.

65. Ibid., 86.

66. Ibid., 85.

67. *Mitchell v. Wells*, 37 Miss. 235, 238 (1859).

68. Ibid., 239.

69. Ibid., 248.

70. Ibid., 249.

71. Ibid.

72. Ibid., 256. See also Miss. Rev. Code, ch. 33, § 3, art. 9 (1857), MDAH.

73. *Scott v. Sandford*, 60 U.S. 393 (1857).

74. *Mitchell v. Wells* (1859), 259, citing to *Scott v. Sandford*.

75. Ibid., 265 (Handy dissenting opinion).

76. Ibid.

77. Ibid., 270.

78. Ibid., 276–77.

79. Ibid., 279–80.

80. Ibid., 285.

81. Ibid.

82. *Leiper v. Hoffman et al.*, 26 Miss. 615, 616 (1853).

83. Ibid., 620.

84. Ibid., 620, 621.

85. Ibid., 621.

86. *Mitchell v. Wells* (1859), 281 (Handy's dissent).

87. Letter, at 58, *Mitchell v. Wells* (Chancery, 1857), MDAH.

88. Ibid., 9.

89. Miss. Rev. Code, ch. 33, § 3, art. 10 (1857), MDAH.

90. 1860, Cincinnati Ward 15, Hamilton, Ohio, roll M653_977, p. 323, image 38, www.ancestry.com.

91. Act of 21 Feb. 1854, ch. 334, 1854 Miss. Laws 460, MDAH.

92. Act of 20 Jan. 1860, ch. 202, 1860 Miss. Laws 259, MDAH.

CHAPTER FIVE
The People of Barnwell against the Supreme Court of South Carolina: The Case of Elijah Willis

1. South Carolina Department of Archives and History, hereafter SCDAH.

2. *Jolliffe v. Fanning,* 10 Richardson 186, 187 (S.C., 1856).

3. *Eighth Census of the United States, 1860* (New York: Norman Ross, 1990), vol. 1, table 2, p. 452.

4. Petition, S165015 no. 28 (1860), SCDAH.

5. *Willis v. Jolliffe,* 11 Rich. Eq. 447, 493 (S.C., 1860).

6. Ibid.

7. Ibid.

8. Ibid., 494.

9. Ibid., 495.

10. Ibid.

11. Ibid., 498.

12. Ibid., 500, deposition of Willison B. Beazley.

13. Ibid., 494, testimony of Pender.

14. *Willis v. Jolliffe,* 496.

15. Ibid., at 504, testimony of James M. Gitchell.

16. Ibid., at 508, testimony of Edward Harwood.

17. Ibid., at 507.

18. Ibid., at 505.

19. A. E. Keir Nash, "Negro Rights, Unionism and Greatness on the South Carolina Court of Appeals: The Extraordinary Chief Justice John Belton O'Neall," 21 *South Carolina Law Review* 141 (1969): 175.

20. *Willis v. Jolliffe* at 409, testimony of Andrew H. Ernst.

21. Ibid. at 494, testimony of Pender.

22. Ibid., 499.

23. Barnwell County Estate Papers, *Elijah Willis*, bundle 126, pkg. 7, SCDAH. Amy was listed as a slave, but based on Willis's actions, that status in his view might have been a formality.

24. *Willis v. Jolliffe,* 501.

25. Ibid.

26. Ibid., at 503.

27. Ibid., at 504.

28. Ibid.

29. Ibid., 494.

30. Town of Williston Official Website, <http://www.williston-sc.com/Intern/H3EarlyDays.htm>, accessed 1 Feb. 2008.

31. *Willis v. Jolliffe,* 492. See appendix 3 for information about some of the signatories of the 1860 Barnwell petition.

32. Ibid., 492.

33. Conveyance Book, Barnwell District, book HH, p. 210 (1854), reel C5401, SCDAH.

34. *Eighth Census of the United States, 1860.*

35. Barnwell County Estate Papers, *Elijah Willis*, bundle 126, pkg. 7, SCDAH.

36. General Assembly Petitions, S165005 #32, SCDAH.

37. There were provisions in the law, however, for the punishment of "any slave or free person of color . . . who shall commit an assault and battery on a white woman, with intent to commit a rape." There was no corresponding statute that protected women slaves. John Belton O'Neall, *Negro Law of South Carolina* (Columbia, S.C.: John G. Bowman, 1848), ch. 3, § 7, p. 29, University of South Carolina Law Library.

38. David J. McCord, 7 Statutes at Large of South Carolina 459, Act of 1800, no. 2236 (S. Johnston, Columbia, S.C., 1840), University of South Carolina Law Library.

39. Id., Act of 1800, no. 1745 (S. Johnston, Columbia, S.C., 1840).

40. See appendix 3 for a discussion of manumission cases resolved at the magistrate court.

41. See for example Christine A. Desan, "The Constitutional Commitment to Legislative Adjudication in the Early American Tradition," 111 *Harvard Law Review* 1381–1503 (1998), or Laura Jensen, *Patriots, Settlers, and the Origins of American Social Policy* (New York: Cambridge University Press, 2003).

42. Records of the General Assembly, Henry Ravenel Petition, undated, SCDAH S165015, no. 1712.

43. Records of the General Assembly, Petition Ex Parte George Bellinger, SCDAH, n.d., S165015, no. 1804, and S16505, n.d., no. 782. It is unclear whether this was the same George Bellinger who emancipated various slaves according to the entries in the Barnwell manumission book. In the entries, this George Bellinger is described as being of St. Bartholomew's parish, which was part of the Charleston district. Colleton was next to Charleston.

44. Ibid.

45. Ibid.

46. Eds. Loren Schweininger and Robert Shelton, *Race and Slavery Petitions Project*, legislatures, 1777–1867 (Bethesda, Md.: University Publications of America), accession nos. 11382703, 11382704, reel 10. See also David Martin petition, Records of the General Assembly, 10 Nov. 1827, S165015 and Records of the General Assembly, Report of the Committee on Emancipation, S165005, 1827, no. 154, SCDAH.

47. Fifth Census of the United States 1830 (National Archives Administration: Washington, D.C.), M-19, roll 169, p. 123.

48. See Court of Equity Records, Edgefield County, ED112, roll 4; ED133, roll 843, SCDAH.

49. Race and Slavery Petitions Project, accession no. 11383702.

50. Records of the General Assembly, Report of the Committee on the Petition of Wm. B. Farr, John Ryan and Wm. N. Mitchell, 5 Dec. 1823, S165005, #228, SCDAH.

51. Records of the General Assembly, Report of the Judiciary Committee on the Petition of Jeremiah Dickey, 4 Dec. 1830, S165005, 1830, no. 21, SCDAH.

52. See appendix 3 for census details on some of the 1860 signatories.

53. John Belton O'Neall, *Biographical Sketches of Bench and Bar of South Carolina*, vol. 1. (S. G. Courtenay & Co., 1859), xvi, University of South Carolina Law Library.

54. *Willis v. Jolliffe*, 11 Rich. Eq. 447, 516 (1860).

55. Acts of 1820 and 1841 cited in O'Neall, *Negro Law of South Carolina*, 11; see also 7 Statutes at Large of South Carolina 459, Act No. 2236, ed. David J. McCord (Columbia, S.C.: A. S. Johnston, 1840), for a copy of the Act of 1820. O'Neall, *Negro Law of South Carolina*, 12.

56. 7 Statutes at Large of South Carolina 440, ed. David J. McCord (Columbia, S.C.: A. S. Johnston, 1840), no. 1745.

57. Ibid., 11.

58. Ibid., ch. 1,, § 43, p. 12.

59. See *Farr v. Thompson, Executor of Farr*, Cheves 37–49 (S.C., 1839).

60. Records of the General Assembly, Judiciary Committee Report, reel s165005, 1818, no. 70, n.d., no. 2572, SCDAH.

61. See O'Neall, *Biographical Sketches*, xviii–xxii.

62. See 7 Statutes at Large of South Carolina 440, ed. McCord, no. 1745.

63. *Farr* at 47.

64. Race and Slavery Petitions Project, accession nos. 11384005 and 11384006, reel no. 11.

65. Ibid.

66. Ibid., no. 11384005.

67. Ibid.

68. Ibid.

69. 7 Statutes at Large of South Carolina 154 (Columbia, S.C.: T. S. Piggot, Printer to the House, 1858), no. 2836.

70. O'Neall, *Biographical Sketches*, xviii.

71. *Carmille v. Adm'r of Carmille*, 2 McMullan 454, 471 (S.C., 1842).

72. O'Neall, *Negro Law of South Carolina*, ch. 2, § 35, p. 22.

73. A. E. Keir Nash, "A More Equitable Past? Southern Supreme Courts and the Protection of the Antebellum Negro," *North Carolina Law Review* 48 (1970): 197–242, 236.

74. O'Neall, *Biographical Sketches*, xv–xvi.

75. Ibid., xvi.

76. A. E. Kier Nash, "Negro Rights, Unionism, and Greatness on the South Carolina Court of Appeals: The Extraordinary Chief Justice John Belton O'Neall," 21 *South Carolina Law Review* (1969): 141–90, 178.

77. Maximilian LaBorde, *A Tribute to Hon. J. B. O'Neall, LLD: Being a Summary of his Life and Labours* (Columbia, S.C.: J. W. Duffie, 1872), 9, South Caroliniana Library, University of South Carolina Archives. Note that O'Neall died in 1863.

78. Gazette Office, *An Address on Female Education, delivered at the request of the Johnson Female Seminary at Anderson, South Carolina* (Anderson, S.C.: 3 Aug. 1849), South Caroliniana Library, University of South Carolina Archives.

79. Edward L. Ayers, *Vengeance and Justice: Crime and Punishment in the 19th-Century American South* (New York: Oxford University Press, 1984), 19. See also Bertram Wyatt Brown, *Southern Honor: Ethics and Behavior in the Old South* (New York: Oxford University Press, 1982), 297, 308, 311.

80. Elijah Willis Estate Papers, bundle 126, pkg. 7, 7 Feb. 1861 inventory, SCDAH.

81. Barnwell County Conveyance Book, vol. NN, pp. 83–84 (1861), reel C5404, SCDAH.

82. Barnwell County Conveyance Book, vol. PP, pp. 208–9 (1863); Barnwell County Conveyance Book, vol. QQ, pp. 73–76 (1864), reel C5405, SCDAH.

83. Petition of Amy Ash and Clarissa Sloan for Letters of Administration, etc. Barnwell County Probate Records, 4 July 1870, Elijah Willis, bundle 184, pkg. 12, reel N1765, SCDAH.

84. See appendix 3 for information on the various sales.

CONCLUSION
The Law's Paradox of Property and Power:
The Significance of Geography

1. Ariela Gross, "Beyond Black and White: Cultural Approaches to Race and Slavery," 101 *Columbia Law Review* 640, 643 (2001).

2. Ibid., 643.

APPENDIX THREE
Supplementary Information Regarding *Willis v. Jolliffe*

1. David J. McCord, ed., 7 Statutes at Large of South Carolina, no. 670, § 1, p. 397 (Columbia, S.C.: A. S. Johnston, 1836–41), University of South Carolina Law Library.

2. John Belton O'Neall, *Negro Law of South Carolina* (Columbia, S.C.: John G. Bowman, 1848), ch. 2, § 4, p. 17.

3. Ibid., § 11, p. 18.

BIBLIOGRAPHIC ESSAY

BECAUSE THE SCHOLARSHIP ON SLAVERY in the antebellum South is voluminous, this bibliographic essay makes no attempt to provide a comprehensive listing of works relating to the topic. Instead, it aims to identify secondary sources that were useful in researching and writing this book. To understand the historical context of this study, it is important to have a sense of the cultural trends and intellectual currents of the time, which in turn impacted questions of slavery, local and national politics, and the law. Alexis de Tocqueville, *Journey to America*, trans. George Lawrence, ed. J. P. Mayer (New York: Anchor Books, 1971), is the most important source for understanding American life during the mid-nineteenth century. Rush Welter, *The Mind of America, 1810–1860* (New York: Columbia University Press, 1975), and Harry L. Watson, *Liberty and Power: The Politics of Jacksonian America* (New York: Hill & Wang, 1990), explain the significance of Whiggery and Jacksonianism. To gain an understanding of legal thought during this time period, consider Lawrence M. Friedman, *A History of American Law*, 2nd ed. (New York: Simon & Schuster, 1985); William Wiecek, *The Lost World of Classical Legal Thought: Law and Ideology in America, 1866–1937* (New York: Oxford University Press, 1998); Stephen M. Feldman, *American Legal Thought from Premodernism to Postmodernism: An Intellectual Voyage* (New York: Oxford University Press, 2000).

The political debates over slavery quickly degenerated into acrimony during the course of the nineteenth century into the eve of the Civil War. Various texts explain slavery's significance in this tension, for example, Michael Perman, *The Coming of the American Civil War* (New York: Houghton Mifflin Company, 1992). Ronald G. Waters, *American Reformers, 1815–1850* (New York: Farrar, Straus and Giroux, 1996), ties the rise in abolition to reform movements, and Jon Butler, Grant Wacker, and Randall Balmer, *Religion in American Life: A Short History* (New York: Oxford University Press, 2003), present an opposite view, the way in which southerners used the language of religion to justify their institution of slavery.

So how then, did these perspectives on slavery develop into a law of slavery? Thomas R. R. Cobb, *An Inquiry into the Law of Negro Slavery in the United States of America*, vol. 1 (Philadelphia: T. & J. W. Johnson,

1858), a treatise written by a southerner, provides a comprehensive explanation of the legal underpinnings for the institution. Various scholars have provided analyses of the law of slavery: Mark V. Tushnet, *The American Law of Slavery, 1810–1860: Considerations of Humanity and Interest* (Princeton: N.J.: Princeton University Press, 1981); Thomas D. Morris, *Southern Slavery and the Law, 1619–1860* (Chapel Hill: University of North Carolina Press, 1996).

How did elite men of the South view slavery? How did they justify it as a practice? Henry Wiencek, *An Imperfect God: George Washington, His Slaves, and the Creation of America* (New York: Farrar, Straus & Giroux, 2003), points to the paradox of elite male freedom fighters of the revolutionary period supporting their right to own slaves. Adam Rothman, *Slave Country: American Expansion and the Origins of the Deep South* (Cambridge, Mass.: Harvard University Press, 2005), explains the development of slavery in the Deep South and the role of revolutionary era elites in contributing to its spread there. William Kaufman Scarborough, *Owners of the Big House: Elite Slaveholders of the Mid-Nineteenth Century South* (Baton Rouge: Louisiana State University Press, 2003), presents a study of who the elite were: large landowners who wielded much political and social influence.

Judges sitting on appellate courts in the antebellum South are an integral part of this study. Various authors explore their role as umpires in negotiating rights in a slave regime: A. E. Keir Nash, "Fairness and Formalism in the Trials of Blacks in the Trials in the State Supreme Courts of the Old South," 56 *Virginia Law Review* 64–100 (1970); A. E. Keir Nash, "Reason of Slavery: Understanding the Judicial Role in the Peculiar Institution," 32 *Vanderbilt Law Review* 7–218 (1979); Reuel E. Schiller, "Conflicting Obligations: Slave Law and the Late Antebellum North Carolina Supreme Court," 78 *Virginia Law Review* 1207–48 (1992); William E. Wiethoff, *A Peculiar Humanism: The Judicial Advocacy of Slavery in High Courts of the Old South, 1820–1850* (Athens: University of Georgia Press, 1996); Timothy S. Huebner, *The Southern Judicial Tradition: State Judges and Sectional Distinctiveness, 1790–1890* (Athens: University of Georgia Press, 1999). Paul Finkelman, *An Imperfect Union: Slavery, Federalism and Comity* (Union, N.J.: Lawbook Exchange, 2000), in turn describes the way in which diverging perspectives on slavery affected how courts in the North and South dealt with manumission. These approaches to manumission could fuel in turn testators' strategic use of geography as discussed in this book.

Other texts explain the significance of geography from the perspective of receiving jurisdictions like Ohio and the efforts of abolitionist lawyers there who effectuated manumissions: Stephen Middleton, *The Black Laws: Race and the Legal Process in Early Ohio* (Athens: Ohio University Press, 2005); Nikki M. Taylor, *Frontiers of Freedom: Cincinnati's Black Community, 1802–1868* (Athens: Ohio University Press, 2005); and Bernie D. Jones, "Southern Free Women of Color in the Antebellum North: Race, Class, and a 'New Women's Legal History,'" 41 *University of Akron Law Review* 763–798(2008).

What light might elite male perspectives on slavery shed on how testators who crossed the color line were viewed? Jan Ellen Lewis and Peter S. Onuf, eds., *Sally Hemings and Thomas Jefferson: History, Memory and Civil Culture* (Charlottesville: University Press of Virginia, 1999); Annette Gordon-Reed, *Thomas Jefferson and Sally Hemings: An American Controversy* (Charlottesville: University Press of Virginia, 1997); and Joshua D. Rothman, *Notorious in the Neighborhood: Sex and Families across the Color Line in Virginia, 1787–1861* (Chapel Hill: University of North Carolina Press, 2003) explain why studies of white men matters in the context of a book on slavery, manumission, and inheritance rights. African American oral history has long realized the significance of white men as fathers of mixed-race enslaved children providing a foundation for a pre–Civil War black elite, even though mainstream scholars were unwilling to do the same: Gail Lumet Buckley, *The Hornes: An American Family* (New York: Alfred A. Knopf, 1986); Sarah L. Delany and A. Elizabeth Delany, with Amy Hill Hearth, *Having Our Say: The Delany Sister's First 100 Years* (New York: Dell Books, 1994); Shirlee Taylor Haizlip, *The Sweeter the Juice: A Family Memoir in Black and White* (New York: Simon & Schuster, 1994); Carrie Allen McCray, *Freedom's Child: The Life of a Confederate General's Black Daughter* (Chapel Hill, N.C.: Algonquin Books, 1998); Josephine Boyd Bradley and Kent Anderson Leslie, "White Pain Pollen: An Elite Biracial Daughter's Quandary," in *Sex, Love, Race: Crossing Boundaries in North American History*, ed. Martha Hodes (New York: New York University Press, 1999); Mark Perry, *Lift Up Thy Voice: The Grimke Family's Journey from Slaveholders to Civil Rights Leaders* (New York: Viking Penguin, 2001). On the other hand, recent scholarship on southern slaveholding families indicate a willingness to explore the interracial nature of white and slave families in the antebellum period: Edward Ball, *Slaves in the Family* (New York: Farrar, Straus & Giroux, 1998); Henry Wiencek, *The Hairstons: An American Family in Black and White* (New York: Saint Martin's

Press, 1999); Edward Ball, *The Sweet Hell Inside: A Family History* (New York: William Morrow, 2001).

In thinking about the ways in which rhetoric about family mattered, the law, of course, was significant. Ideas about family, who could be family and who could be enslaved, date to the early colonial period and the way in which elites used the law to demarcate a line around whiteness and white families: Kathleen M. Brown, *Good Wives, Nasty Wenches, and Anxious Patriarchs: Gender, Race, and Power in Colonial Virginia* (Chapel Hill: University of North Carolina Press, 1996). The "one-drop" rule meant that all blacks, regardless of their white ancestry, were always to be considered black, and enslaved women passed their slave status onto their children: David Hollinger, "Amalgamation and Hypodescent: The Question of Ethnoracial Mixture in the History of the United States," 108 *American Historical Review* 1363, 1379 (2003); Peter W. Bardaglio, "'Shamefull Matches': The Regulation of Interracial Sex and Marriage in the South Before 1900," in *Sex, Love, Race: Crossing Boundaries in North American History*, ed. Martha Hodes (New York: New York University Press, 1999), and Werner Sollors, ed., *Interracialism: Black-White Intermarriage in American History and Law* (New York: Oxford University Press, 2000). Michael Grossberg, *Governing the Hearth: Law and the Family in Nineteenth Century America* (Chapel Hill: University of North Carolina Press, 1985), and Margaret A. Burnham, "An Impossible Marriage: Slave Law and Family Law," 5 *Law and Inequality* 187–225 (1987), provide in turn, a means of developing comparisons between white families and black enslaved families under the law. The former were granted greater protections over the latter.

Sources that explore the apparent fluidity of race relations between blacks and whites in Louisiana include Mary Gehman, *The Free People of Color of New Orleans: An Introduction* (New Orleans: Margaret Media, 1994); L. Virginia Gould, "Urban Slavery—Urban Freedom: The Manumission of Jacqueline LeMelle," in *More than Chattel: Black Women and Slavery in the Americas*, eds. David Barry Gaspar and Darlene Clark Nine (Bloomington: Indiana University Press, 1996); Sybil Klein, ed. *Creole: The History and Legacy of Louisiana's Free People of Color* (Baton Rouge: Louisiana State University Press, 2000); Judith Kelleher Schafer, *Becoming Free, Remaining Free: Manumission and Enslavement in New Orleans, 1846–1862* (Baton Rouge: Louisiana State University Press, 2003); Jennifer M. Spear, "Colonial Intimacies: Legislating Sex in French Louisiana," 60 *William and Mary Quarterly* January 2003 http://www.historycooperative.org/journals/wm/60.1/spear.html (1 Feb. 2008). This perception of fluid race relations has led to the argument that mixed-race slaves and free blacks found it easier to inherit from white male partners and fathers. But the evidence indicates that race still mattered and that the retention of white wealth within white families was paramount.

These differences between the treatment of white and black families were built further on a foundation of gender and the sexual exploitation of enslaved women: Eugene D. Genovese, *Roll, Jordan, Roll: The World the Slaves Made* (New York: Vintage Books, 1976); Harriet A. Jacobs, *Incidents in the Life of a Slave Girl*, ed. Jean Fagan Yellin (Cambridge, Mass.: Harvard University Press, 1987); Elizabeth Fox Genovese, *Within the Plantation Household: Black and White Women of the Old South* (Chapel Hill: University of North Carolina Press, 1988); Edward E. Baptist, "'Cuffy,' 'Fancy Maids,' and 'One-Eyed Men': Rape, Commodification, and the Domestic Slave Trade in the United States," 106 *American Historical Review* 1619–50 (2001).

Adrienne D. Davis, "The Private Law of Race and Sex: An Antebellum Perspective," 51 *Stanford Law Review* 221–88 (1999), is an earlier treatment of this topic of inheritance rights for the enslaved partners and children of slave owners, but this book offers a more in-depth study. It builds on Ariela J. Gross, *Double Character: Slavery and Mastery in the Antebellum Southern Courtroom* (Princeton, N.J.: Princeton University Press, 2000), in exploring cases of contested wills as another arena where slavery and mastery in the courtroom came into play, exposing the tensions between owners' competence as slave owners and slaves' agency. Helen T. Catterall, *Judicial Cases Concerning American Slavery and the Negro* (Washington, D.C.: Carnegie Institute, 1926–37) provides a catalog of reported cases from the appellate courts of the antebellum South and a means of identifying cases to study.

Kitty v. Commonwealth, 94–95,
175n106
Knotts, William, 132
Kyler and Wife v. Dunlap, 94

laches, 87
laws, 98–99; changes in, 67; inheritance, 15, 64; sexual-offense, 22;
slavery, 13–14, 17–18, 43–44,
96–97. *See also* legislatures;
manumission laws
lawsuits: commercial, 16
lawyers, 138–40
Leah et al. v. Young and Shackleford,
76, 172n32
Lee, George Hay, 26–28
legacies, 26–28; to children, 54; to
slaves, 83
legal culture: of the South, 99
legislators: attitudes of, 108
legislature: Kentucky, 72–74, 96;
Mississippi, 101–9, 117–18
legislatures: and abolitionism,
106–7; and courts, 127; and
emancipation, 80–81; and manumission, 49, 103–9, 134–35;
petitions to, 49, 125–26; role
of, 100–101, 120; state, 2; and
trusts, 142
Le Grand v. Darnall, 23–24, 166n5,
166n8, 166n10
Leiper v. Hoffman et al., 121–22,
177n82
Lopez's Heirs v. Mary Bergel (f.w.c.),
60, 169n63
Loring, Israel, 108–9
Louisiana, 18–19, 57–67; inheritance laws of, 64; judges in, 67;
Supreme Court of, 60
Louisville Chancery Court, 88

*Lucy Thomas and others v. Nathaniel J.
Palmer,* 47, 168n11
Lumpkin, Joseph, 53–54
Lyne, Edmund, 74

Macarty v. Mandeville, 60–61,
170n64
Major v. Winn's Adm'r, 91–92,
174n92
Mallet v. Smith, 50–51, 168n24
Mandeville family, 60–61
manumission: in 1820s, 103–4; in
1830s, 103–4, 108; in 1840s,
108; banning of, 118; conditions
of, 28–29; before death, 40; and
legal system, 22; liberalization
of, 73–74; prerequisites for, 25;
procedures for, 135; rejection of,
108. *See also* emancipation
manumission laws, 5, 48–54, 73,
134–35; changes in, 16–17, 19;
flexible, 86–87; tightening of,
89–90
marriage, 66, 129
Martin, David, 137
Martin, François-Xavier, 65
Maryland, 23, 33–34
masculinity, 42
mastery, 12
McIsaac, John, 69
McKibben, James, 142
McKinney, Robert J., 51–52
McMinnis, Polly, 79
Meaux, John Woodson, 82
mental capacity, 35
Miles, Frankey, 26–28
miscegenation, 10, 126–28
Mississippi, 52, 117–18; and free
blacks, 57, 102, 112, 117; free
people of color in, 54–55;

petition: Barnwell manumission, 125, 133–35, 138; in state legislature, 103–9
Pigeau v. Duvenay, 65, 170n81
Pool, Ephraim, 37–39
Pool's Heirs v. Pool's Executor (1858), 167n50
Pool's Heirs v. Pool's Executor (1859), 38, 167n51
population: of Barnwell, South Carolina, 127; of free blacks, 93
power: of enslaved women, 8–9; of judges, 5
precedents, 99
prejudice, 37–39
Preston, Isaac T., 61–62
Prevost v. Martel, 66, 170n87
Pringle, George, 48–50
privilege, 150, 152–54
professionalism: of lawyers, 139
property: safeguarding of, 40; slaves and, 45; slaves as, 73, 83; and whiteness, 7
property rights, 3–4, 20, 38; and free blacks, 149; and judges, 154; of slaves, 143–44; testators', 6; and whites, 7, 61, 152

quadroon ball, 58

racial: hierarchy, 109–10; mixing, 55; stratification, 13
Ravenel, Henry, 135–36
Rawlings, Isaac, 28–29
Rawlings, William Isaac, 28–29, 36
Ray, B., 92
Read, J. Harleston, 134
Reed's Will, 70, 171n7
reenslavement, 124
Reeves, Maria, 95

relationships: familial, 119; nature of, 8–9
religion, 4
reputation: of slave owners, 35
requirements: for emancipation, 88–89, 93. *See also* bonds
revocation: of wills, 24–25
rights: of free blacks, 110–11; individual, 119; inheritance, 98–99; of parents, 70; of slave owners, 141; of slaves, 34, 62–63, 81–82, 143–44. *See also* property rights
Ring, Rebecca, 83–84
Robertson, George, 30–31, 68–72, 75–82; and fraud, 83–84; and manumission, 76–78; and paternalism, 78–79; and slavery, 84–86
Robinett v. Verdun's Vendees, 170n81
Rost, Pierre A., 65–66

Samuels, Green B., 25–26
Sanders v. Ward, 53–54, 169n32
Scott v. Sandford, 118–19, 177n73, 177n74
secessionism, 100, 102–3
sexual-offense laws, 22
Sharkey, William L., 55
Shaw v. Brown, 117, 169n45, 177n47; facts of, 56–57; and *Mitchell v. Wells,* 112–13. See also *Mitchell v. Wells*
Shelby County Court, 28
Simpson, James, 34–35
Sinnet, Anna, 59–60
skin color, 58, 137
Slaughter, Gabriel, 78–79
Slaughter, John H., 78–79
slave owners: attitudes toward, 42; reputation of, 35; rights of, 141